THE FINE ART OF
SELLING
BECAUSE EVERYONE SELLS

THE FINE ART OF
SELLING
BECAUSE EVERYONE SELLS

RULES FOR UNLOCKING YOUR POTENTIAL

ED MAXWELL

ISBN: 979-8-9907952-0-4

Printed in the United States of America

CREDITS:
Cover Photo: Shutterstock/Montri Thipsorn
Cover Design & Formatting: Lisa Monias

"A diamond is just a lump of coal that stuck to its job."
— Leonardo Da Vinci

For my patient wife, Linda, who listens to my pitches,
and my patient partner, Joe, who listens to my rants.

TABLE OF CONTENTS

INTRODUCTION: THE Fine Art of Selling................................... 1

PART ONE: Passion, Empathy and Product Knowledge............... 7

CHAPTER ONE: Passion 9

CHAPTER TWO: Empathy....................................... 15

CHAPTER THREE: Product Knowledge 23

PART TWO: Tactics and Strategies for Sales Success.................. 29

CHAPTER FOUR: Sales is a Performance Art........................ 31

CHAPTER FIVE: Urgency 41

CHAPTER SIX: Eleven Extra Steps 57

CHAPTER SEVEN: The Internet of Things 67

CHAPTER EIGHT: Without Sales, Everything Stops! 81

CHAPTER NINE: Collaboration 101

CHAPTER TEN: So You Think No One's Watching... 109

CHAPTER ELEVEN: Asking the Right Questions 117

CHAPTER TWELVE: HUNGER!!! 125

CHAPTER THIRTEEN: First Impressions Matter a LOT 131

CHAPTER FOURTEEN: "I Hate Salesmen" 139

CHAPTER FIFTEEN: Rules for a Successful Sales Career 167

CHAPTER SIXTEEN: PostScript: The Master Salesperson 195

ABOUT THE AUTHOR 199

INDEX 200

The Fine Art of Selling

Selling is an underrated profession. A good salesperson will always find a job because a good salesperson knows how to sell the boss as well as the customer. It doesn't matter whether you're selling refrigerators, used cars, or God to parishioners, selling is the fine art of demonstrating that you have a solution that will make their lives better. The purpose of this book is to bring my four decades of experience in selling to anyone interested in learning this fine art.

I was once at a restaurant and ran into some friends. I was introduced to someone I didn't know and he asked me what I do for a living. I replied that I was in sales. He replied, in a very condescending manner, that he "guessed someone has to do it." This comment was from a minister who, if he's doing his job right, is selling all the time. Everyone who wants to be successful sells. People who want to be very successful sell well. This book is dedicated to the fine art of selling. I hope that my passion for selling will demonstrate itself in these pages.

In our world today, success is often measured not just by the quality of your products or services but by your ability to persuade, to connect, and to convince. Sales is the lifeblood of commerce, the invisible force that propels economies forward and transforms ideas into reality. *Without any sales, it all comes to a halt.* This maxim applies to job seekers, as well as parents, teachers, and workers in an auto factory. Everyone needs to know how to sell.

This book is your guide to understanding the fine art of selling, to harnessing the power of persuasion, and to unleashing your potential as a top-notch professional. Whether you're a long-time sales veteran looking to refine your techniques, are just starting to embark on this exciting journey, or someone who understands that selling oneself or one's ideas is critical to success, you'll find valuable insights, strategies, and principles within these pages.

We'll cover psychological subjects like "empathy," discuss the art of effective communication, and delve into the need to build lasting relationships with your clients, whether these clients are parishioners, retail customers or business people. We will get into the basics of relationship building and the difficulties of objection handling. Our purpose is to equip you with the knowledge, skills, and mindset necessary to excel in your world, whatever that world is.

This book is not about increasing your sales numbers or increasing your income. It's about mastering the art of ethical persuasion in a very competitive world. It's about learning techniques to be successful in whatever line of work you're in.

I believe strongly that the sales profession is not about manipulation or coercion, but rather about understanding the needs of your clients or customers in order to deliver genuine value that you yourself believe in. Sales is the job of everyone who wants to live in this competitive world—whether you're competing for a job or trying to be better at the job you have. Everyone needs to understand sales techniques in order to succeed at whatever they do.

I hope you will take this journey with me. I hope you will discover ways to be a better person, to understand that selling underlies everything we do. I hope you come away from reading this book with an understanding that sales is about becoming a trusted advisor, a problem solver, and a source of inspiration. By the time you finish reading this book, you will be well on your way to becoming a person who doesn't just close deals but opens doors to opportunities and success; and a person who realizes that the fine art of sales is essential in every walk of life.

I will be using the word "salesperson" to describe anyone who is trying to convince a boss, or client, or student, a parishioner, or child, that their idea is the best solution to whatever the issue is. In this book, we are all "Salespeople."

There are 10 things every salesperson (I.e. every person) should say to themselves as they brush their teeth each morning:

1. I will work to be better today than yesterday.
2. I will make what is important a priority.
3. I will cultivate deeper connections.
4. I will stay positive no matter what.
5. I will keep pushing boundaries.
6. I will refuse to take failure personally.
7. I will help as many people as I can today.
8. I will appreciate people.
9. Everything I do will be grounded in integrity.
10. I will live in gratitude.

So, please proceed with an open mind and take notes.

Part One of this book will discuss the three essential require-ments for anyone looking to succeed in sales: Passion, Empathy, and Product Knowledge. Part Two will present strategies and tactics for being successful in sales.

Passion, Empathy and Product Knowledge

CHAPTER ONE

Passion

Passion is defined in Webster's Dictionary as an "intense, driving, or overmastering feeling or conviction" (www. merriamwebster.com.) Passion is an enthusiastic attachment to something: a particular activity, a sports team, a hobby, cause, or person. It often goes beyond mere liking or enjoyment and is identified by the following characteristics:

Passion is not "passing" or temporary and is often accompanied by a willingness to invest time, effort, and energy into the object of passion. People are willing to go above and beyond to pursue what they are passionate about. Passionate people are committed people.

Passion is Internally Motivated: Passionate people engage in their chosen activity or pursuit because they genuinely love it, not solely for external rewards or recognition.

Passion is Enduring: Passion is not a short-lived infatuation but a long-term and consistent dedication to something that remains a source of inspiration and satisfaction over time.

Passion is Personally Fulfilling: Pursuing one's passion often leads to a sense of personal fulfillment and satisfaction. It can be a source of happiness and purpose in life.

Passion is a very interesting characteristic. Someone can be very laid back and seem uninterested and uninteresting, but when you bring up a particular subject that turns them on, they can go on for hours. As a result, passion can manifest in various areas of life, including hobbies, career, relationships, creative endeavors, sports, and social causes. It's a driving force that compels individuals to excel, innovate, and make a meaningful impact in their chosen domain. Passion can vary from person to person, and what one person is passionate about may differ greatly from another's passion. It is a deeply personal and subjective experience that plays a significant role in shaping an individual's identity and life choices.

Passion is absolutely critical to success in sales. It's a belief in your product and its benefits, and a desire to communicate this belief to others (customers, clients, parishioners, children, etc.)

Mark Ruffalo plays a Boston Globe writer, Michael Rezendes, in the movie "Spotlight." This was a very powerful movie, but what stood out for me was Ruffalo's characterization of a very passionate journalist.

Ruffalo portrays a journalist with true passion--the kind of passion that a good salesperson needs; the passion that comes from belief in your cause--in a salesperson's case, the cause is your product.

So how do you get passionate about your product?
I have sold industrial products, like air compressors, for example, throughout my sales career. My technique is to find the features and benefits of the product that I can be passionate about: the efficiency, the volume of air produced per horsepower--whatever. I find it and I'm passionate about it because I know it can improve a manufacturer's capacity or reduce costs—in general, it solves problems.

Another product I've sold throughout my selling career are fiberglass tanks. Through most of my career I sold one brand and then, because of circumstances, changed brands. How do you change your passion for one into a passion for another? By understanding the manufacturing process and how it is better; by understanding the company and the company's service--going beyond the materials in the product to all the "bones" that make one company different from another.

If you can't feel the passion about your product or service, then you can't *sell* the product.

So, it's not just the generalized notion of passion--but the ability to be passionate about what you're selling. Product knowledge can be taught; even empathy can be worked on; passion cannot be taught.

You know what you're passionate about. I have a friend who gets very passionate about the subject of fusion; another who is passionate about rock bands. But can you be passionate about refrigerators and air compressors? Can you be passionate about Subaru's or a house you have to sell as a realtor?

Passion for selling as a career--not a job to create income for your true passion (whatever it may be) is the first step on this path. Passion for your product--truly believing that it is better than the competition's, that it serves an important function for your customer, that you truly believe in it--is critical to success as a salesperson.

Passion for your product arises out of product knowledge and knowledge of your competitors' products. Passion for your product arises out of knowledge of your customer's business and how your product can improve your customer's business, or lifestyle in the case of a consumer product.

As a consumer, you can "feel" passion--when a salesperson believes in what they are selling. That passion arises out of confidence in their product knowledge and confidence that they understands you as a customer. Passion is the leg that the stool must have to support your weight.

CHAPTER TWO

Empathy

In its simplest definition, empathy is the ability to put oneself in another's shoes; the ability to understand and share the feelings, perspectives, and experiences of another person, to see the world from their vantage point, and to genuinely connect with their emotional state. Empathy is a fundamental aspect of human interaction and is essential for building strong, positive relationships and for fostering understanding and compassion.

Before getting into sales, I was a teacher. And, as a teacher, I believed one thing absolutely: if a student didn't understand what I was explaining, it was NOT the student's fault. It was mine. I always questioned the teacher who blamed the students for not understanding the subject matter they were teaching.

All while I was teaching, I was watching the students' eyes. If

I saw blankness, I knew I was on the wrong track and needed to change direction. A student's bad grade was result of my not understanding where this student was at intellectually.

A great salesperson gets into the shoes of their customers--literally. A great salesperson is not "pushing their product." A great salesperson is ultimately a teacher trying to understand the needs of the student (the "customer") and only then working with the customer to make sure the product solves the problem.

The route to greatness is to really understand your customer. You are the teacher, they are the student. And if your "pitch" elicits blank stares, you are going down the wrong road and need to evaluate yourself. You have a product and you need to be able to explain how it benefits them. And if they don't believe it benefits them (if the stares remain blank), then blame yourself and fix the pitch or move on.

A few years ago, I was tutoring a young man for his High School Equivalency test. He was struggling with math, but loved go-cart racing. So, I started from that position: "you have a one-mile track, your go-cart goes 10 miles per hour. How long will it take to go around the track." He answered in seconds. And, as we changed the track length and the speed of the go-cart, each time he computed the answer instantly. I got into his shoes and he succeeded.

Maybe, you're dealing with a Facilities' Manager of a manufacturing plant, or a husband and wife looking for a refrigerator or house, or a parishioner dealing with grief. What are their issues? How can you help resolve these issues?

You've heard this before: "don't sell products, sell solutions." But you can't sell solutions if you don't know what the problems that your customer is facing.

So, now change the scope of your task: who is my client; what does this person do in the company; what are their issues; what are the company's problems; how can my product help them. Get to deeply understand your customer, like understanding the young man who didn't think he understood math, but did, in fact, when it was related to something he was passionate about: go-cart racing.

This need to know your customer is required no matter what you're selling. Homeowner says "I need a new refrigerator." How you respond is critical. "What is it you like about your current fridge?" "What things would you like in a new one?" And the response tells you everything: "Oh, I want the freezer drawer on the bottom and I want double doors and I want it counter deep." Now you're getting somewhere, and your customer appreciates your concern.

You're selling oil water separators, and the plant manager has a problem with equipment leaking oil. You need to get into the plant and understand the problem, and only then can you recommend a solution. Does the separator need to manage the whole facility, or can it be placed close to the leaking equipment? Can one large separator solve the problem, or a few smaller ones which are easier to install and may be less expensive?

I'm familiar with a company that manufactures a product that measures the permeability of packaging materials. This is a very sophisticated, technical sale. There is absolutely no way to sell this product without understanding how important air-tight packaging is to particular customers. Potential customers may be more or less interested in the permeability of their packaging. You need to find out who in the company is responsible for testing packaging permeability? There are many questions that the salesperson must ask themselves before even talking to the customer for the first time. However, the core requirement for the salesperson is understanding how important the testing procedure is and how perfectly the product you're selling performs that function.

Get into your customer's or client's shoes. Be empathetic to their problems. Make sure you're talking to the right person. And only then can you propose a solution.

The salesperson who sits in an office and never visits the customer will never understand (read "empathize") their needs or the urgency of their requests.

Real sales is "eyeball to eyeball:" Looking into your customer's eyes, recognizing their needs and then, and only then, proposing a solution. The questions are: how can your ideas benefit the client and how can you solve the particular problem your customer or client has with the products or ideas you're selling?

A self-absorbed salesperson is an oxymoron. A self-absorbed salesperson cannot succeed. A great salesperson must put the customer first, not the sale.

Psychologists recognize three types of empathy: Cognitive empathy, emotional empathy and compassionate empathy. We will only concern ourselves with cognitive empathy, as essential to the sales process;

Cognitive Empathy: Along with passion, this a salesperson's next most important trait. It's the is the ability to understand another person's perspectives. It allows you to "get inside their head" and grasp their point of view without necessarily sharing their emotional state. Cognitive empathy is often crucial in problem-solving and conflict resolution. A salesperson with cognitive empathy tries to understand the client or customer or student's perspective or issue and has a desire to help solve a problem or issue. You don't have to feel what they feel, but you do have to understand where they're coming from.

Talk to your customers, clients, student, children one on one and understand where they're coming from. If you're not willing to do that, you won't be able to sell your idea or product.

Harper Lee, in her book "To Kill a Mockingbird," wrote a line for Atticus Finch, the lawyer: "You never really understand a person until you consider things from his point of view. Until you climb into his skin and walk around in it."

This idea has been worked and overworked. "You don't know someone until you walk a mile in his shoes" is another way to put it. But this is more than a phrase--it's a deeply, deeply true statement. You can't understand your customers' motivations, you can't understand your manager's motivations, you can't understand what your boss is looking for--nothing makes sense unless you can truly get out of your skin and get into the other person's skin. This is a very demanding idea.

Salespeople are typically driven by their egos--by necessity since we have to take so much rejection.

But ego is something we have to let go of because it stands in the way of getting into our customer's mind.

What are your customer's needs, personally and corporately? How do they "sell" your product to their bosses and make themselves look valuable in the boss's eyes? Selling should not be transactional--it should be solutional--a solution for the customer, for his company, for you, the salesperson. Leave your ego (and your cell phone) at the door and try to truly understand what the customer, what your customer's boss, what your boss, and what the people around you, want.

Walk a mile in their shoes.

CHAPTER THREE

Product Knowledge

When you ask a real estate agent what makes a property valuable, the answer is always: "location, location, location." When you ask a customer what makes a one salesperson better than another, the answer is always--"product knowledge, product knowledge, product knowledge."

Most salespeople who have been selling a product for some time feel that they possess product knowledge. But product knowledge is an elusive beast.

Let's take an item like a refrigerator. They seem to be a commodity. But what makes one better than another? Assume you're a Sub-Zero salesperson. You have to convince the prospective customer that there's a value to paying several times more for the Sub-Zero than for a Kenmore or Maytag. What's the value in a Sub-Zero? Now is when product knowledge plays a critical role. You need to understand refrigeration compressors. What makes one compressor better than another? What is the advantage of two compressors, since Sub-Zero has two compressors and normal refrigerators have one. Sub-Zero has two evaporator coils and dual zone temperature control. What does an evaporator coil do? Why is dual zone temperature control important? Why does a Sub-Zero weigh twice as much as any other refrigerator? Why is this important? What do people want in a refrigerator? Adjustable shelves? Easy access to the freezer?

This is what's involved in "product knowledge." When a salesperson says: "Oh, yeah, Sub-Zero is the best. Everyone knows that," the salesperson is not selling, they're just taking up space, giving a bad name to the sales industry. They are not practicing the fine art of selling.

So, first you must know your product, inside and out. Then you have to know your competitors' products inside and out. Then you make presentations to anyone who will listen in order to practice your "pitch."

And speaking of "pitch," every salesperson should have a 5 sentence "elevator speech" about themselves and their product. This is the five sentences that gets a customer to stop and listen. These are the five sentences that demonstrate to the customer that you know what you're talking about. And this "elevator speech" applies to everyone who wants to practice the fine art of selling.

An example of an elevator speech from a Sub-Zero salesperson might go like this: "My name's Ed and I've been selling Sub-Zeros for five years now. There's a reason they're the highest priced refrigerator on the market. You don't have to worry about failure--everything is dual: dual compressors, dual evaporators. And the reason they weigh twice as much as the other refrigerators is the insulation--so they are tremendously energy efficient. It would be worth your while to spend a few minutes while I show you the benefits of a Sub-Zero."

Let's look at the value that product knowledge plays in the selling process.

Product Knowledge builds trust: Customers are much more likely to have confidence in a salesperson who demonstrates a thorough understanding of the product they are selling. When salespeople can answer questions and address concerns about the product, it builds credibility and confidence in the product.

Product Knowledge allows for clearer communication of the features and benefits of the product, allowing the salesperson to tailor the presentation to the customer's needs.

Knowledge of your product as well as your competitor's products allow the salesperson to overcome objections or concerns when making a purchase decision. Salespeople who know their products well can address these objections with relevant information about their product and the competitor's and provide insight into why their product provides the right solution which increasing the chances of closing the sale.

By understanding a customer's needs and by having a deep knowledge of your product, the salesperson can identify opportunities for possibly moving the customer into a new direction with another product in your product mix. A good example of this would be a car salesman. I have a friend who recently bought a new car. They went into the dealership and said "this is the model I want." My friend was ultimately unhappy with the purchase because the salesperson didn't identify the needs of this particular customer. My friend wanted a car that sits "high" on the road. However, they got a sports car with a lot of road noise and, for an older person, this was unacceptable. The salesperson stopped at "sitting high" and didn't understand to total needs of the customer.

So, to summarize what we have discussed
Product Knowledge:
1. Boosts a salesperson's confidence, making them more persuasive and enthusiastic when presenting the product to potential buyers.
2. Allows the salesperson help customers solve problems and

find the best solutions. This customer-centric approach can lead to long-term relationships and repeat business.

3. Can educate customers about how the product can meet their specific needs, which is particularly important for complex or innovative products.

4. Helps minimize mistakes or inaccuracies in information provided to customers, reducing the risk of customer dissatisfaction and returns.

Allows salespeople to perform better and achieve higher sales targets. They can close deals more efficiently and effectively.

PART TWO

Tactics and Strategies for Sales Success

CHAPTER FOUR

Sales is a Performance Art

Performance arts are wonderful. You rehearse for weeks; you have a dress rehearsal to prepare for the performance; then you perform--perhaps many times--in front of an (hopefully) approving audience that gives you a standing ovation after the final curtain.

Sales is a performance art, but the audience never applauds. A scowl may more often the reaction of your performance. Sales is a solo art. The sales performance is primarily between you and your client.

It's very easy to get down on yourself, especially if the sales aren't coming and the reward doesn't equal the effort that you're putting into it.

So what do you do when you hit a dry spell? What happens if the sales don't equal the effort that you're putting into it? What happens when your boss starts asking you where the orders are? What happens when your job application is rejected? How do you deal with rejection? How do you deal with an audience that doesn't applaud.

Like any performing artist who doesn't get the applause they expected, the first job is to look within yourself for some of the answers. Don't blame the audience. Look within.

Are you doing everything you can do to get those sales?
1. Is your product knowledge up to date?
2. Is your pitch honest and clear?
3. Do you really believe in your product(s)?
4. Do you believe in yourself and your abilities?
5. Are you passionate about what you're selling?

If you don't believe in yourself and your product, you will never convince the customer to believe.

Once you've answered those questions, honestly, you know where you need to focus.

All sales start with a *belief in yourself* and your product. (In a recent interview, even Liza Minnelli confessed that she had to learn to believe in herself and the song before she could sing it successfully.)

All sales start with *an intimate knowledge of yourself and your products.*

If you're deficient in either of these--believing in yourself and your product--fix it.

Let's look at the sales process as a performance art in detail:

The Stage: The stage is wherever the sales process is to take place: your house, your office, your boss's office, a retail store, a pulpit, Zoom—wherever.

The Script: The script is essential to the sales process, whether it's memorized, internalized or written, the script outlines what you need to convey to the potential customer, the key points you want to emphasize, and how you plan to address objections or questions. We often go into a situation thinking that we'll be able to handle it without preparation. Not the case. Every situation needs preparation. Every situation needs a script.

The Actor: Performers adopt a character when they step onto the stage. In sales, dishonesty is often readily apparent. A good salesperson is always themselves; a good salesperson projects confidence, empathy, and a genuine desire to help the customer, creating an honest character that the audience can identify with.

Delivery: Delivery is so important in every aspect and is discussed at length in this book. The fine art of delivery includes tone of voice, body language, and the ability to adapt and react to the audience's reactions and needs. An effective salesperson requires emotional intelligence to connect with customers on a personal level.

Engagement: I'm always looking at the client's eyes, whether an individual or a group, to see if they're grasping what I'm saying or have lost interest. A person's eyes will tell you all you need to know.

What are the techniques to keep a client or class engaged? It could involve using storytelling, active listening, and the ability to respond to the customer's cues and feedback. And all of this involves extensive preparation and understanding what you selling and who you're selling to. All of which will be discussed in this book.

Improvisation: By improvisation, I mean being able to think on your feet when a question or objection is raised. Much like a live performer who can't predict every twist and turn in a performance, salespeople encounter unexpected situations and objections. Understanding your audience and understanding your product, and watching the performance of the experts, are essential to the skill of improvisation.

Creating an Impact: Every performer wants to create an impact—get a standing ovation. What is the impact that the salesperson is looking for? That the client or audience understands your position, that all their objections and questions have been answered. When a person feels understood, valued, and emotionally connected to the salesperson and the product or service, they are more likely to make a purchase.

Feedback and Adaptation: I discuss the debriefing process several times in this book. Looking back on your performance and being honest with yourself is essential to improvement. It is not a weakness to ask the customer or audience what you did right and what you may have done wrong and how you can become better.

The Grand Finale: Of course, the standing ovation in the selling process is closing the deal. Just as a standing ovation is the highlight of a performance, successfully sealing the deal is the ultimate goal of the salesperson whatever form that success takes: your customer buys the refrigerator, your child agrees to do what you ask, your parishioners keep coming back.

In essence, the sales process as a performing art highlights the fine art of selling: the importance of charisma, empathy, persuasion, product knowledge, and adaptability in the salesperson's role, all of which are critical to creating a memorable and successful sales performance.

When you're confident in yourself and excited about your products, you're unbeatable.

Unforced Errors: Many golf and tennis sports announcers refer to what they call "unforced errors." Unforced errors are errors that are made in just about any sport that would not be made under normal circumstances. A basketball player coming down the court unchallenged misses a layup. In tennis, your opponent hits a nice shot to your forehand and you bang it into the net. You should have made the shot.

In golf, if you hit a tee shot into the middle of the fairway, 100 yards from the green, and you slice it into the woods, that's an unforced error.

A recent article I read by golf pro, Tom Patri, discusses "unforced errors" in golf. (www.thegratefulgolfer.com/2021/03/15).

Eliminating unforced errors can apply to the sales profession as well. As Patri says "Through the years, I've watched a number of shots carelessly thrown away—not due to a player's skill level—but due to one's inability to either manage their emotions, the course, or both."

Over the years, I have seen this very thing in our sales profession. Unforced errors result in lost sales and these lost sales may happen, not because of a salesperson's skill level, but because of one's inability to manage the course (product knowledge), managing one's emotions, and understanding the customer's needs.

One example in Patri's article is the golfer who hits a poor shot and makes an unforced error by trying to hit a great shot to recover from the bad one. As Patri says, "You didn't get in this position because you were in control of your ball. What makes you think you can thread the needle in your recovery shot? Play back to safety."

We, as salespeople, need to understand ourselves, our motivations, our customer's requirements, and always play within ourselves.

You've just left a sales call and you realize that you started off totally wrongly. Maybe you made assumptions about the customer's likes and dislikes, or needs, or issues and now the customer is angry or just withdrawn.

Don't try to correct the situation by putting yourself in a worse position. Play back to safety. Make a new appointment. Start over. Admit your error, apologize and get back into play. The customer will respect you for that.

I once played in a music group and when the lead singer and guitarist started the set by playing all the wrong chords, he then blamed it on the fact that it was a new guitar and he wasn't used to it. We were all embarrassed by his unforced error and the fact that he didn't just apologize and start over. Trying to explain what you did wrong is not an apology. Never try to justify your error. Apologize and fix it.

I believe very strongly in this statement: when your gut tells you that things aren't going right, believe your gut. And then fix it. Get back into play. Don't stick your head in the sand and hope it all works out. Admit your error, fix the issue, apologize, get back into the game and get the sale.

Email is the Worst Way to Communicate!
You've heard the saying many times: "free is not free." There's a cost to everything. Well, the same can be said for email. Email is free and there's a horrible cost related to the free email: inundation. We are inundated by emails. They get lost in the shuffle. You know the conversation: "did you get that email I sent you?" "What email? I get 100 emails a day. How do you expect me to pick yours out from the bunch?" And some folks get many more than 100--probably hundreds.

According to statistica.com the forecast is that, by 2025, more than 376 billion emails will be sent globally every single day. So, as a salesperson, do you think you have a chance finding and communicating with customers by email? The future for communicating by email is almost gone, and will only get worse. What are the alternatives? What do I say to someone who says "they aren't responding to my emails."

Call. What a shock. Pick up your cell phone and call.

But when you do that, you better have your pitch prepared. There are two ways a call gets answered: by voice mail or by the customer directly. And you'd better be ready to have a good 30 seconds prepared or you'll never hear from them again. I know sales reps who just say: "This is John Jones. Please give me a call back." This will never get a call back.

Get a pitch, a good pitch. Try it out on spouses and friends. You have to state your name, return phone, company, and the reason why the customer should return your call--and make it a good, strong reason. "I represent a manufacturer of industrial air compressors and we have stock and can ship immediately. It's an excellent product and outperforms the competition. I can't wait to hear from you. Remember, high quality, great pricing and in stock."

Get back on the phone. It's worked for decades and it beats email.

If you have the customer's cell phone, *try texting*. Use this carefully. Always give the customer an option to opt out and always put your name in the first line and use the customer's first name in your intro.

And use your text for a good old pitch. "Joe. This is Ed Maxwell. Sorry for texting you but I really need to tell you about the line of industrial air compressors we represent. And they're in stock! Just reply STOP if you don't want to discuss this, but I'd really like 5 minutes of your time. Give me a call."

Use LinkedIn. Find your customer's profile. Try to connect with them. Send them an email--again with your pitch. Never forget your pitch--sometimes called a Value Proposition. (See the section in this book on Value Proposition.)

The bottom line--email is dead. Be creative, use another way.

CHAPTER FIVE

Urgency

Customers don't want to wait. When they need one of your products or services, they typically need it right away. The salesperson's job is to understand that urgency. The longer the customer waits for you to get back to them, or provide them with the information they need, the more likely that the order will be lost to the salesperson who recognizes the urgency.

Understanding a customer means understanding the customer's needs. The need may be a quotation so that the product can be budgeted. The need may be a drawing or specification so that the engineer can spec your product into the project.

Everyone reports to someone up the chain of command. It's important for the sales rep to understand that when someone asks you for something, it's because someone up the ladder wants the information--urgently. Without the quote, without the specifications, without the lead time information, the order gets lost to someone who recognizes the urgency.

In this time of supply chain delays, it's up to the sales rep to stay in touch with the customer--to keep the customer informed about the timing for whatever their current needs are. The corollary to Urgency is Communication. Remember, again, everyone answers to someone up the corporate ladder. The more you communicate with your customer, the better the your contact looks to the bosses.

The underlying principle that will allow you to stay in communication with your customer, is to make follow-up lists.

No More Excuses: Write it Down!!! Keep a Bullet Journal:
In my almost 50 years in sales, I can't tell you how many times I've asked someone if they did something and the response was: "I forgot." The simplest way to solve this problem of forgetting seems to be the one that people resist like the plague: keep a list; write it down; look at the list every day.

There is a movement becoming hugely successful in the U.S. almost overnight, called *"Bullet Journals."* "Track the Past, Order the Present, Design the Future" is their value proposition. Ryder Carroll is the inventor of this enormously popular organization scheme. While the concept is simple (using pen and notebook), the critical component of this idea is that you have to spend time reflecting on the journal--what are your current tasks; where are you headed. Writing things down is not the end point; reflection on what you wrote is the end point. Hundreds of thousands of people are using Carroll's method. Check it out: www.bulletjournal.com.

I use an online system called Todoist (www.todoist.com)

I can forward emails right to Todoist that I need to see later, put reminders on these emails or notes; create notes and reminders and take notes, typed and handwritten, right onto the app. I have been using Todoist as my "bullet journal" for years. But putting something somewhere is meaningless if you don't spend time reflecting on your notes: what got done (delete it)? what got delayed (change the reminder to a new date)? what needs to be done by someone else (forward it)?

But what if you don't want to use computers or smartphones to help remember things.

Sometimes, It seems absolutely impossible to keep up with it all. Family demands, company demands, customer demands--how to keep it all under control is a huge issue today. And, despite having dozens of things to remember, if you forget ONE thing, that's what everyone gets mad at you for. But there's no excuse for forgetting anything these days.

So I'm going to tell you what I do. First thing is that I always have a notebook. And all my notebooks have integrated pen loops with pens inserted. (Notebooks aren't much good without a pen.) More recently I have begun to use a Rocketbook, which allows me to wipe a page clean when the project is done. (www.rocketbook.com)

I can't tell you how many times I have heard--"sorry, I forgot." There's no excuse for forgetting in this age of memory apps. I hate it when I'm the one who has to remind the supplier--"hey, where's my quote." There's no excuse.

Write it down on paper; ask Siri or Google Assistant to remind you; type it into Todoist, or make your todo list a widget on your phone.

And stop making excuses--darn it.

Don't Be A Lazy Salesperson:

Selling is best when it's done face to face. Why?

Face-to-face sales allow for a highly personalized interaction. You can see the customer's eyes and determine if you're getting through. You can tailor your approach to the individual customer's needs, preferences, and pain points, creating a stronger connection and increasing the likelihood of a successful sale.

Face to face selling builds trust which is a fundamental aspect of sales. Meeting in person allows the salesperson to establish trust through their body language, tone of voice, and overall demeanor. This trust is often harder to establish using virtual methods.

Sales is a relationship business. Face to face selling allows you to build rapport with a customer, which is crucial for closing deals. Face-to-face interactions allow for small talk which can help in understanding the customer's needs and objections better and ultimately lead to a more successful sale.

I find that it's harder for a customer to say "no" when you're there in person. In-person sales allow salespeople to immediately address customer objections and concerns. They can provide real-time answers and solutions, which can be more effective than using virtual options.

It's easier to demonstrate your product or go over literature in person. Whether it's a test driving a car or taste-testing a food product, the physical presence of the customer and the product can be essential to making a sale.

A lawyer friend once told me that they liked to get the "smell of the room." This is so important in the sales process. Whether you're selling a refrigerator to a husband and wife, or an air compressor to the plant engineering staff, a significant portion of communication is non-verbal, including body language, facial expressions, and tone of voice. In-person sales allow both the salesperson and the customer to pick up on these cues, which can help in understanding and conveying information effectively.

A very important side effect of face-to-face selling is that long-term business relationships are often built on personal interactions. Face-to-face meetings can help in establishing and nurturing these relationships, which can lead to repeat business and referrals.

However, it's important to note that while person-to-person sales have their advantages, they are not always the most efficient or cost-effective method for every product or market. Many industries and products have successfully embraced online sales, telemarketing, and other remote sales methods. The choice of sales approach depends on the nature of the product, the target audience, and the overall sales strategy.

Classification of Sales Approaches

As an observer of sales people, I have come to classify the sales approach into three large categories.

1. Relational Sales
2. Transactional Sales
3. Route Sales

Although I tend to favor relational sales, there is a time and place for each type.

A *relational salesperson* puts the relationship above capturing the order. If the product doesn't fit the customer, the relational salesperson will tell the customer that the product won't fit his needs and lose the sale. Sales managers don't tend to like this type. My brother was the finest personal example of relational salesperson. When he died, tragically, in 2004, hundreds of people traveled hundreds of miles to his funeral. He was all about relationships and his sales were spectacular.

A *transactional salesperson* is all about getting the order. This is the aggressive "closer" that books are written about. For the transactional salesperson, making money and pleasing bosses is primary. The attitude of the transactional salesperson is: "I'll never see this customer again, so I need to make this sale and go on." A good analogy is the automotive assembly line. Phrases like "sales is a numbers game" is common among transactional types.

A *route salesperson* is a person with established customers who buy specific products and they need and want to be seen on a regular basis. If it's the first Tuesday of the month, the route salesperson is at ABC, Inc. Every first Tuesday of every month. Examples of route sales types are SnapOn or Matco tools sales people. Many salespeople fall into the route salesperson trap.

Transactional Sales: If you've ever been to a timeshare sales event, you know what a Transaction salesperson is. The Transaction Salesperson knows (or thinks) they'll never see you again, so anything if fair game--play on your guilt, play on any weakness he's been trained to spot. They know this is a one-time shot and that sales is a numbers game: talk fast and furious to enough people, and you'll land your quota.

So, the transaction salesperson is a popular style in situations where there is a one-time event with virtually no chance of seeing the customer again, so anything goes. Beware of The Transaction Salesperson.

Never put your sales team into a situation where they feel that getting the sale is all there is.

This style can be a danger to a commission only sales team. If one's living is solely determined by commission, if the only way a salesperson can survive is to close the deal--then you may be inadvertently creating a Transaction Salesperson. A salesperson has to be able to make a living with a base salary; a salesperson has to be able to pay for gas and expenses with an allowance. If not, they may, of necessity, turn into a Transaction Salesperson and hurt your company's reputation.

Route Sales: A route salesperson does something that's very important in the sales process: keeps in contact with customers on a regular basis. A route salesperson sometimes gets a bad rap.

But they perform an important, essential function for some companies and something that all companies need to put into their repertoires. The route salespeople that immediately come to mind, as I mentioned above, are SnapOn, Matco tool, etc. sales folks. This group also includes liquor salespeople, potato chip distributors, soft drink distributors, etc. The lesson we can learn from the route sales folks is that we need to keep in constant and regular contact with the customers who order from us again and again.

Do NOT neglect your good customers, thinking that they'll always be with you. There's another salesperson lurking in the background who wants your customer's business. Beware of taking customers for granted.

Relational Sales: Some years ago, I bought a used car. Used car sales folks have a bad reputation. They often get a very low rating on the professions scale. My salesman, Calvin, called me, faithfully, three times a year: on my birthday, on Christmas, and in the early spring. He had no agenda other than to say hello and to stay in touch. But where will I buy my next car?--from Calvin. Any salesperson, no matter what they're selling, can be a relational salesperson. Calvin personifies the sales profession: future sales generated from relationships. I'm not talking about taking the customer out to dinner or inviting his family to your house for a cookout. I'm talking about caring for the customer and communicating this concern to them. I'm talking about making the customer think that it's more than the order that is at stake. That you're in this for the long term and that you'll take care of them long after the order is placed and shipped.

Building relationships with customers is crucial for sales-people for several reasons:

Strong relationships often lead to customers staying with your business longer, increasing the value they provide over time.

A long-term relationship with a customer is the direct opposite of "churn." The opposite of "churn" is loyalty.

Improved Customer Loyalty: Loyal customers are more likely to return to your brand over others to make purchases. Loyalty that's built over time with consistent, positive experiences.

Building customer loyalty to you as a salesperson means that, should you have to change brands for some reason, your customer will stay with you and trust that you will continue the consistent, positive experiences with the new brand.

When customers feel valued and heard, they are more likely to provide constructive feedback, which can be invaluable for improving products and services.

Customers who trust you will provide references and allow

you to build your business with new customers.

In essence, for salespeople, building strong customer relationships is not just about making a sale; it's about creating a loyal customer base that feels connected to the brand, leading to sustainable business growth.

The Value Proposition was the centerpiece of a sales presentation I recently gave to a networking workshop.. My focus was the "elevator speech"--the speech that you give when someone asks you what you do for a living; the speech that the listener gives you thirty seconds to deliver and rolls their eyes when you never get to the point. The centerpiece of the elevator speech is the Value Proposition.

Wikipedia defines a value proposition as "a promise of value to be delivered, communicated, and acknowledged. It is also a belief from the customer about how value will be delivered, experienced and acquired. A value proposition can apply to an entire organization, or parts thereof, or customers accounts, or products or services."

The value proposition of the products or service that you sell are the things that distinguish them and separate them from the competition--what is often called the features and benefits. The value proposition can also be the benefits that you bring to the sales process or the organization that you represent. The value proposition is a statement summarizing why someone should use your product or service over anyone else's. It is absolutely essential that you think about this and internalize it and practice it and use it every chance you get. It doesn't need to be long--in fact, it should be short and to the point and represent the soul of who you are and what you're selling.

Some examples:

Uber, the car service: 1. Pickup in less than 5 minutes; 2. Lower prices than a taxi; 3. An app to track your car's approach; 4. Cashless transaction; 5. A rating system that guarantees security. "Tap the app, get a ride."

Slack, the messaging service: "A Messaging App for Teams who put robots on Mars." And "All your tools in one place." Evernote, an online note storing app: "Remember everything." "Provides the ability to organize all your notes in one place so you never forget a great idea."

What is the essence or the soul of your business or service? Once you have determined that, put it into as few words as possible and internalize it and use it until it becomes a part of you. Every business and every product should have a value and every employee should understand and buy into that value; every person should have a value and should be able to vocalize that value and believe in that value.

This idea is worth thinking about--long and hard. What is

your value? What is your company's value? What is their product's value?

People tend to believe in a person or product that has value. People tend to buy a product or service from a person who believes deeply in what they're selling and can express that value briefly and confidently and from the heart.

Customer Centered Selling: Four Important Steps:
Customers must be at the heart of any sales process. I have discussed previously about relational selling versus transactional selling. Transactional selling is not customer-centered, by definition. For a transactional salesperson getting the order is more important than doing right for the customer; meeting sales goals supersedes making the customer happy. Relational selling is customer centered. Relational salespeople know that they will live with the results of the sale and therefore they make sure the customer is well-served.

Everything these days is becoming "customer centered." Netflix "learns" what you like to watch and features the programs similar to ones that you have watched in the past. Amazon "learns" your buying history and "suggests" things that you might like. The future of selling is knowing your customer better than your competition does and being able to use that knowledge to service them better, to make sure your customer gets the solution that is best for their needs.

Four things to do before making your first sales call on a new customer or even your second and third call on an old customer:

1. Look up the company on any search engine, like Google or Bing. This will give you an overview of the company's ownership and number of employees.

2. Go to the company's website. If there's an "About" tab, click on it. Learn everything you can about the company--websites are great sources of insight into the company's culture, no matter how large or small the organization.

3. Go to LinkedIn and look up the company's president and any of the people that you're meeting with. LinkedIn gives tremendous insight into a person's interest, if they are keeping up their profiles.

4. Check other social media outlets to get even more insight. Does the company post on Social Media (Instagram, Threads, X) feed? A Facebook page?

Putting yourself into a selling situation without knowing everything you can about the customer you're trying to sell is like coming up to bat with a broomstick. You may hit the ball, but you've reduced your odds by a whole lot.

Do your homework. Get to know your customer before making your pitch and tailor the pitch to the customer's needs.

CHAPTER SIX

Eleven
Extra Steps

Battling wind gusts up to 60 mph, dragging a sled weighing hundreds of pounds, Louis Rudd and Colin O'Brady, separately and alone, with no outside help, crossed the Antarctic recently. O'Brady won the "race," completing the journey in 54 days; 56 days for Rudd. The trip was 925 miles covering approximately 16 miles a day. Some days they couldn't see their hands in front of their faces. The amazing thing is that they are the only two to survive this journey and they did it at the same time. But that is not the lesson here.

For a lot of us, every day seems like a journey across the Antarctic--pulling a 300 pound sled and battling 60 mph winds.

Walking 15 miles a day means pushing forward one step at a time, 30 steps a minute, counting every step, struggling for every step. And when Rudd was exhausted for the day, when he couldn't take another step, he took eleven more steps.

Why eleven? It was once calculated, Rudd explained, that if the famous English explorer, Robert Falcon Scott and his team, had taken 11 more steps each day of their expedition in the early 1900's, they would have survived.

When you're tired, and you need to get one more quote done, make one more sales call, answer one more customer service question, satisfy one more customer's urgent request--remember: Eleven More Steps. Success demands Eleven More Steps. There is no easy way. Hook up your 400 pound sled and drag it Eleven More Steps.

No one is bigger than the team!

According to reporting by ESPN, Patriots' coach Bill Belichick and quarterback Tom Brady got into a little back and forth argument. Belichick was complaining, according to the report, about Brady's sloppiness in a recent game—poor completion record, a couple of interceptions, etc. And of course, Brady is a superstar with five SuperBowl rings and wasn't having any of it. Belichick is reported to have told Brady "No one is bigger than the team."

What a lesson for all of us: no one is bigger than the team.

No matter what team we're on—a sports team, a business team, a sales team, an educational team—we're all on a team of some sort. In fact, we may be on several teams.

It's very easy, especially when we're successful, to think that it's all about us—I did that, I accomplished that, it's all about me. But it never is. A lot of people help all of us get where we are. A lot of people sacrifice many things to allow us to succeed: our spouses, our parents, our children, our bosses, our employees, the folks sitting behind the desk making our lives a little easier.

It's time to start each day by telling ourselves "I am not bigger than the team." And it's time to start thanking the team for what they do to help us achieve our goals.

"Charlie Hustle" Pete Rose:

"I'm not the type of player who's going to be 'Johnny Hustle'," so says the baseball player who's too good to run every hit out. The original hustling baseball player was Pete Rose, nicknamed "Charlie Hustle." So, what is this hustle all about?

The Urban Dictionary defines "hustle" this way: To have the courage, confidence, self-belief, and self determination to go out there and work it out until you find the opportunities you want in life.

Hustle is the heart of sales. A good salesperson never dogs it, never stops selling--is always hustling. If you're not hustling, you're not selling. If you're not hustling, you're never going to the top.

If you're not hustling every single day, finding new customers, learning more about your product, servicing your existing customers--if you're not doing this every single working day, then you're not hustling. Plan your work and work your plan--at full speed, every single day.

If you believe in what you're doing, hustle comes naturally. Be proud of your profession; be good at what you do, and never stop hustling.

A-B-C = Always Be Closing:

Alec Baldwin, in the 1992 movie, "Glengarry Glen Ross," made the line "Always Be Closing" famous. The classic formula for salespeople has always been--make your presentation, then ask for the order. I have a business associate friend who I nicknamed "The Closer" because he's always closing, no matter what's being discussed. By the time "The Closer" is done selling, the customer is wondering why he even considered anyone else or any other product.

When you ask a real estate agent what the most important thing to consider when buying a property, the answer is always LOCATION, LOCATION, LOCATION. And when you ask a true salesperson what they most important quality of a top performer is CLOSE, CLOSE, CLOSE.

There is no top performer of any sport or profession who is not always on, always thinking about how to perform better, how to achieve absolute perfection.

Selling is a profession as honorable as any and no one engaged in this profession should ever sell themselves short. As an honorable profession, those who are salespeople should do everything possible to perform at the top of their capabilities. Stand tall as a salesperson; be proud of your profession; never apologize--but ALWAYS BE CLOSING. There is absolutely nothing wrong with asking for the order.

As a consultant, I always tell clients: don't present a problem or situation without also suggesting a solution. The solution is the "close." If you're a politician, you end a speech by asking for the vote. If you're a preacher, you end by asking for the "Amen." If you're in sales, you end your pitch by asking for the order, by finding out what the objections may be, and resolving them until the order is placed.

Selling is Teaching and Never Forget That:

Think about what you liked about your favorite teacher from grade school, high school or college. I can pretty well guess what you liked: The good teacher cares and shows that fact by connecting with you--especially with the eyes. I went to a doctor recently and noted that, during the time he was with me, he only looked at me three times. The rest of the time his eyes were locked onto his computer screen. A good teacher connects with the students with eye contact. A good salesman does the same.

Another thing that identifies a good teacher is knowledge of the subject. A student can tell immediately whether a teacher knows what he's talking about. Product knowledge is critical to good sales.

Good teachers ask questions to make sure the students understand what they're taught. A couple of thousand years ago, a Greek philosopher name Socrates, developed a method of teaching we now call the Socratic method. It involves using questions and answers to arrive at an understanding. Good teachers use this method to help students understand a subject. Good salespeople should use the same approach. Don't come into the sales situation with an answer--come in with questions and let the customer arrive at the solution.

Remember how, as you were growing up, you said to yourself that when you're a parent, you won't do this or that that your parents did and you didn't like.

Think that way as a salesperson. What do you like about that car salesperson you deal with; what don't you like. Learn from watching and observing.

Become a good teacher and you'll be a great salesperson. Stop pushing for the transaction and start observing; stop talking and listen.

So Is This Digital Stuff Important?

First and foremost, we all have to understand that digitization is not something that we can fight. We are all buying "smart" TVs--and smart TVs are as connected to the internet as are our smartphones. Smart TVs are digitizing our habits--what we watch, when we watch it, in what room we are sitting when we watch--everything! New cars are already "smart" and some new cars have cameras that tell you when you stray from the lane. Digitization is here. Embrace it. Don't fight it.

Second, and just as important, customer relations management (CRM) software is critical to successful management of your future in sales. If you have good, detailed information in your CRM program (we use Sage ACT! in our company), you can send targeted newsletters to your customers or make targeted mailings. There are excellent online newsletter software offerings out there like MailChimp and Constant Contact. Using these packages, you can create a newsletter and email it through their software, as long as you have good email addresses--which, of course, you have because you keep your CRM software up to date.

And last, but not least, understand that the products that you may be currently selling may be talking to each other or may be capable of talking to each other. Use these facts to sell the product. Machine to machine communication is taking place now; machine to human communication is taking place now. There's nothing that any of us are going to do to stop it.

Get on Board--Enjoy the ride!

Don't Be A Luddite!

According to Wikipedia, "The Luddites were a group of English textile workers and weavers in the 19th century who destroyed weaving machinery as a form of protest. The group was protesting the use of machinery in a 'fraudulent and deceitful manner' to get around standard labor practices."

Fast forward to today: Today's Luddites are fighting everything that dominates the business landscape: social media, the internet of things, machine to machine communication, YouTube, and other technologically based innovations. I was at a sales conference recently and many of those in the group that I was in were denying that neither they nor their customers are "into" social media. (In order to completely avoid social media, one would have to hide in the woods of Vermont.) These same folks were selling a preeminent internet of things (IoT) products and were therefore deep into technology without even knowing it. We salespeople need to get on board with IoT, with social media, with LinkedIn. Those who don't will be left behind.

It's everywhere. There's no avoiding it.

I was on LinkedIn recently and saw a posting from one of my connections that led me right to a potential customer, right in my back yard.

We need social media to make connections; we need to understand how the internet of things is going to be (is) part of our lives now and in the future. Embrace it, understand it.

CHAPTER SEVEN

The Internet of Things

As I stated above, the world is about to change--whether it's for the better or for the worse remains to be seen. But we'd better be ready for it. Let's look at an example of what this is all about.

My sales company represents a manufacturer of a product that measures liquid levels in above ground petroleum storage tanks. Each of these product monitors contains a cellular "SIM" card and is, in essence, a cell phone, with a motherboard, antenna. The monitor reads the level in the tank and sends the information via the cell system to a data center. The software in the data center interprets the data and sends email or text alerts as needed to the company dispatchers. If you buy into the whole system, the dispatcher's job can also be "robotized" and everything from reading the tank level to dispatching the tank truck could be handled in the software. This is the "internet of things;" this is the future. And business owners who adopt products like this one are adding tremendous efficiencies and dollars of profit.

But there's one thing that bots lack:
Billionaire, Paul Allen, of Microsoft fame, put up $125M to see if there is some way to inject common sense into these bots. Researchers have spent decades trying to figure out how to program common sense into robots--unsuccessfully. So, what do we bring to the sales process--or rather, what SHOULD we bring to the sales process that will keep us from being replaced by bots: common sense, of course, and deep product knowledge. What exactly does it mean to have common sense? Common sense means having wisdom, insight and awareness. These are not teachable attributes. If you're passionate about what you sell and you believe in what you sell, and you care about your customer and how your product provides a solution, then common sense is embedded into your brain. Common sense comes from experience, knowledge and observation. These are the attributes that a good salesperson must have to be successful:

common sense and deep product knowledge. Everyone has met sales folks who could be replaced by a bot--someone with superficial product knowledge and no common sense. Make sure you're not one of those.

Many things are going to be sold by bots--assisted by chatbots. They make businesses operate more efficiently and productively. As salespeople, we have to recognize the future and make sure we understand how it will impact us. That being said, there are thousands of products that will be sold that involve an intricate knowledge of the product and the subtleties of application--that require common sense. Chatbots will help us locate potential customers and perhaps even narrow down the most likely candidates for our product. And bots will be part of the products that we sell in the future. But bots will not replace a good salesperson--a person with deep product knowledge and the common sense to apply that knowledge.

Here's another final example of how the internet of things will be part of everything we sell and we need to understand how to use it. Industrial air compressors used in manufacturing now ship with data gathering modules that send information via cell towers to service houses so that they can spot problems before they occur or schedule maintenance based on hours of usage. Compressor manufacturers that don't build units with these modules will lose out on sales because customers want to make sure that these key components of manufacturing don't break down and IoT (the internet of things) helps to resolve these issues.

I highly recommend "Digitize or Die" by Nicolas Windpassinger, with an introduction by Jean-Pascal Tricoire, president of Schneider Electric.

The internet of things will revolutionize our lives in much the same way that the telephone, television, airplane and computer did.

Don't fight it. Understand it.

For Bots Sake--What the Heck are "Bots"????
"Bot" is short for "robot" and refers to automated software that resides in almost everything we buy and use these days, from cars to phones to refrigerators and stoves. Bots can be good bots or bad bots depending on who designs them. (If you haven't watched the 1968 movie "2001, A Space Odyssey" recently, you should. Hal is a bot who started good and turned bad.) Bots are really lines of computer code that reside in the software programs and devices that we use every day. If you order a Lyft or Uber car, there's a bot residing on your cell phone showing you exactly where the car is and when it will arrive. Bots are the result of programmers trying to make computers intelligent. Some bots reside within apps, but slowly and surely, bots are replacing apps. What does all this mean for us sales folks and

business owners? Well, Chatbots are the wave of the future and we need to know about them. Siri, Google Home and Alexa are chatbots. We ask questions, they listen and "understand" and respond. Facebook Messenger will be incorporating a chatbot into their system. The future is coming fast. This is the Internet of Things (IofT). This is the digitization of everything. What to do? What to do? The first thing is to be aware of what's going on. The second thing is to know that there are bad bots that can do bad things, like infiltrate your computers or spread lies about your company. But good bots ("Chatbots") are coming closer and closer to simulating human intelligence. Chatbots have already begun taking over customer service jobs, scheduling service and maintenance, scheduling orders and calling customers to tell them their order status. To quote Mark Zuckerberg of Facebook fame: "I don't know anyone who likes calling a business. And no one wants to have to install a new app for every business or service that they interact with. We think you should be able to message a business, in the same way, you would message a friend."

Should we worry?

Interactive chatbots will be programmed to ask questions when a customer calls. For example, if there is a chatbot programmed for an air compressor sales operation, the chatbot would be programmed to ask a caller questions like: "What size is your current compressor? Do you think you need more air? What voltage do you have at your location?" ...and so on and so forth, until the chatbot is ready to quote, place the order and continue following the order to shipment. However, that chatbot can't visit the customer and evaluate the actual needs of the customer. Only a good salesperson can.

Over and over again, I have preached product knowledge and persistence as the keys to success in sales. It's going to become more and more critical that we sales folks, and anyone interacting with customers, have to be smarter than the bots. Our product knowledge cannot be superficial and artificial. BE SMARTER THAN A BOT!

LinkedIn — Back from the Dead:
Last week I attended a two day sales conference and came away with a lot of ideas. One of the huge things that I came home with was a new appreciation of LinkedIn. LinkedIn has always been a place where everyone goes and writes their profiles and then never goes back.

In 2016, Microsoft bought LinkedIn and over the past two years has made it look very much like Facebook. What does this mean for us sales folks?

1. It means that you better get back on and update your profile, fast, 'cause people are looking.

2. It means that you need a business presence on LinkedIn. You can now easily create a Company Page right from your profile page. Just click on "Work" on the top right of the page and a new window will open. Scroll to the bottom and you will see "Create a Company Page +"--and LinkedIn will lead you to the next steps.

3. Get involved. All of your colleagues probably have profiles (they're not updating). Link to them and they'll get the message.

4. Comment, post and make more industry friends. You'll be familiar with the format since it's a lot like Facebook.

5. LinkedIn is Facebook for business. You can find out who's doing what; who moved from one job to another; what's going on in your market place.

6. Finally, you can join groups that specialize in what your focus is. Again, you click on the "Work" tab on the upper right of the page and then click on "Groups" to find a list of groups that fits your profile.

7. At this level, everything is free. But I know sales managers who use LinkedIn premium which costs almost $800 a year.

LINK IN to LINKEDIN

Saban Makes Decision and the Tide "Rolls:"

Sometimes we have to make decisions on the spot to save the

situation. The University of Alabama was in such a spot in the 2018 college football playoffs. The running game wasn't working and the only option for Saban was to play a freshman who was an untried passing phenomenon. In this section, I'm not looking at the performance of the freshman quarterback, I'm looking at the decision making of the coach, Nick Saban.

There comes a time in the sales process when you may realize that you're going in the wrong direction--that you may lose the order if you don't change something. And that change may involve changing your program completely. In the case of Alabama, it meant changing from a running game to a passing game; it meant taking out a running quarterback (Jalen Hurt) who brought the team to the finals with a 25-2 record, with an untested freshman (Tua Tagovailoa), a passing quarterback.

So, here's the situation: you're really close to getting the order, but you know in your gut that something's going wrong and that if you don't change something you may lose it. The customer may be saying that you have the order and everything may point to your getting the order, but you know something is wrong. Or you may be in a situation where you definitely see that the situation is not good.

When that happens, it's time to change the quarterback--it's time to change from a running game to a passing game. It's time to re-think the whole game plan.

I tell everyone I work with: "if you see something, say something." You never know where the insight is going to come from and everyone needs to be empowered to speak up.

I've been in situations where I knew that I rubbed the customer wrong and I needed to back out of the sales situation and let someone else be the lead. Winning the game--getting the order--has to be the driving force, not your ego.

If you think you may lose the order, don't be afraid to change the game plan or even change the quarterback.

Everyday Lessons from Belichick Leadership Rules:

Lesson 1: There is no detail that is too small to pay attention to.

Belichick's coaches analyze every movement of every player of their next opponent. You often hear him, after a game, when the press wants to question him about the game, saying "I'm only interested in next week. This week is over." His only concern is how to beat the next team he plays. And to that end, he has his coaches looking at the opponent's tapes and noting every detail of the opponent's play design. His coaches look at everything--even watching how the opposing quarterback moves his hands or his head prior to a play or how the left guard pulls on a pass play, or how the free safety moves on an end run. In our lives, we tend to ignore the little things. In Belichick's world, it's all about the little things.

Lesson 2: A "mediocre" player is a poorly coached player. Belichick puts the blame for mediocrity right where it belongs: poor coaching. He is often quoted as saying: "Give me someone who wants to work hard, and I'll turn him into a superior player." We often tend to take the easy way and blame the student or the employee for failure, when the blame has to be put where it belongs--on poor leadership, bad coaching, unclear direction. Belichick's lesson for us is "don't blame the player for a bad performance, blame the coach."

Lesson 3: Take responsibility for bad outcomes. After a game that's been lost, or poorly played, Belichick never blames the players. He blames himself for not preparing the players properly or for not giving proper instruction to the coaches. It's very easy to blame everyone but yourself for a failure. Failure on the bottom starts with poor leadership at the top. When you fail, figure out what you did wrong and fix it.

Lesson 4: Never give up--never. Belichick says this over and over again in interviews: never give up. Yogi Berra, during the 1973 pennant race, was the originator of this phrase: "It ain't over, till it's over." In the 2017 Superbowl, the Falcons were winning 28 to 9 going into the 4th quarter. The Patriots scored 19 unanswered points in 4th quarter to tie the game and caused

THE INTERNET OF THINGS

the first overtime in Superbowl history.

The Apollo 13 crew mission motto was "Failure is not an option." We can all take a lesson from this. Hard work and commitment are the keys to winning in the long run. And losses are only short-term setbacks.

Finally, Winston Churchill said: "Continuous effort, not strength or intelligence, is the key to unlocking our potential."

Rejected!

Federick the Great was the legendary King of Prussia (Germany) in the mid and late 1700's. He famously declared: "It's not a disgrace to be defeated. It's a disgrace to be surprised." You have lost an order and you're now analyzing why it was lost. There is absolutely no reason to be dishonest with yourself. Were your sales calls well made, well prepared, and well argued? Honestly? So here are some facts:

According to Steve W. Martin in a recent survey of 230 buyers (www.stevemarting.com)

Buyers rate two-thirds of business to business salespeople as being average or poor:

1. Just 18% of salespeople are classified by buyers as trusted advisors whom they respect
2. Only 31% of salespeople can talk effectively with

senior executives

3. 54% of salespeople clearly explain how their solution positively impacts a customer's business

So what's the problem? According to Martin:

1. Buyers sense the salesperson's agenda to make the sale and can feel pressured ["Transaction Man will do anything for the order"]

2. Salespeople give a canned pitch and don't listen to buyer requirements

3. Differences in communication style and personality can alienate buyers

4. Salespeople don't adapt their approach to differing gender perspectives

5. Salespeople want to develop relationships but buyers are too busy

A poorly prepared sales call in which the salesperson can't answer the customer's questions, can't respond to the competitive issues, and doesn't know how their product applies to the customer's needs, leads to certain defeat. The salesperson has been surprised by poor preparation, has not prepared himself for the battle. This can be prevented three ways: preparation, preparation, and preparation. Know your product, know your competitors' products and know your customer.

There is a lot to be gained from analyzing the lost sale.

Every salesperson faces rejection, sometimes many times a day or week depending on what type of product you're selling. I remember to this day, forty years later, losing a bid on a major project. This was a project that was going to earn me the respect of my boss and my peers. This project was a game changer and would put me over the top on my quota. Back in those days, if you had to call someone, you did it from your car window over a pay phone. I called the customer and asked who had won the bid and found out it was not me. I was shocked. I had done everything right. I had a product that was unique and solved the customer's problem. I lost to a competitor who could not touch the quality of my product. I sat in my car for an hour, unable to adjust to this loss—to my loss. It was a huge project and everyone was looking at it and waiting for me to get the order. Now I had to tell everyone that I didn't get it.

Rejection is such a personal thing for a salesperson. It's never the product that's rejected. It's us. The customer didn't like ME. I did something wrong. What makes a salesperson great is their personal involvement in the sale. What makes a salesperson successful is their personal involvement in the sale. But once the decision is made, once you've done everything possible, everything within your power, and you lose the sale, it has to stop being personal. It now must become analytical.

What to do? Sit down with someone you respect and go over the process and try to figure out what you did that you could have done better.

I have a firm belief that the salesperson who has the relationship with the buyer wins the order. The issue is what exactly the relationship is. The most difficult situation is when the seller (not you) and the buyer are personal friends. That's a hard relationship to overcome. Superior quality and lower price may help, but often the buyer just tells his friend your deal and if the other seller can meet your deal, you lose. More and more, personal relationships can not overcome a better product at a better price, but there are situations when it does and be prepared for rejection. The opposite of that situation is, of course, when you have the personal relationship with the buyer. The real danger here is taking that relationship for granted.

Never assume you have the order until the product has been paid for, no matter how close you are to the buyer. No celebration until the check clears.

CHAPTER EIGHT

Without Sales, Everything Stops!

There comes a time in every salesperson's career (or more accurately, many times), when sales dry up. Manufacturers don't care why the sales have stopped; they don't listen to our excuses (buyers on vacations, economic downturn, etc, etc). They are are solely concerned about backlog and layoffs of key workers--and the blame for this downturn is always placed on sales. "If you did your jobs better, we wouldn't be experiencing this downturn. Get off your rear ends and sell something." So what do we sales folks do when the hammer comes down: "we need more sales or we have to lay off manufacturing personnel?"

To get out of this situation, we need to go back to basics:

1. Start with your existing and past customers. Is what you sold them in need of replacement? Do they need more of what your sold them--has their business grown? Has your product added technology that would benefit your customer? So, take your list of customers and start calling them--*existing customers are the best source of future business.*

2. Next, get a list of customers you lost. There are a lot of reasons the customer who gave the order to someone else may no longer be happy with their decision. Call them; ask the question. That five minutes may be well spent.

3. Get out of your comfort zone! Sales people love to keep going back to the customers who make them comfortable--who accept them and like them. This is one reason why sales dry up. New customers and new markets for your products breathe life into your sales. Find new customers who are in the same business as your existing customers and go see them. Find new markets for your products and get out to see those new potential customers. Use Google; use Bing; use linkedin.com--use technology to find these new customers. *If your existing customers can't provide enough sales to keep the production lines running, then you have to find new customers and new markets.* You can't protect your customers if they can't give you enough sales to make your bosses happy.

4. Never, ever use the excuse that it's the other sales folks who are not pulling their weight. It's on you. Take responsibility. Don't wait for others to pick up the slack. It seems unfair, but sales is responsible for keeping the production line running.

"Without sales, everything stops." Do not take your job lightly. People depend on you doing your job. Take what you do very seriously and do the absolute best you can--families depend on you--and not just your own.

Start by Making Your Bed:

In a 2014 commencement address to University of Texas students, Admiral McRaven offered Ten Life Lessons he said he learned by being a Navy SEAL. I have added my comments to his lessons relating his lessons to the sales process.

Lesson Number One: "If you want to change the world, start off by making your bed."

Why is this task so important? Because if you start the first task of the day by being organized and orderly, that sets the mood for the rest of the day. Making a bed well takes a little time and more discipline than most people realize. Try it and see if it makes a difference. This may not work if your spouse happens to be still sleeping. But the underlying message is to start the day by organizing yourself. It may mean simply sitting at the breakfast table and making a list of your tasks for the day.

Lesson Number Two: "If you want to change the world, find someone to help you paddle."

I have written many times that we cannot be successful in sales by ourselves. We need to seek help, always, because other people see things that we don't and those things help to close sales.

Lesson Number Three: "If you want to change the world, measure a person by the size of their heart, not the size of their flippers."

We are often influenced by things that don't matter and we don't pay attention to the little things that do matter. Take your blinders off and really look at the little things around you; look into a person's heart. Successful salespeople need to understand people and their needs: look into their hearts.

Lesson Number Four: "If you want to change the world, get over being a sugar cookie and keep moving forward. We, in the sales profession, often feel "entitled" to that order--we deserve it because we worked harder than the other guy. Well, McRaven says, get over it and move on. The other sales-person got it and you need to check your ego at the door."

Lesson Number Five: "If you want to change the world, don't be afraid of the circuses."

We live in a crazy world. People make ordering decisions for reasons that we'll never understand. Unexplained failure--the loss of an order for reasons that don't make any sense--will happen over and over. Again, get over it and move on.

Lesson Number Six: "If you want to change the world, sometimes you have to slide down the obstacle head first." The meaning of this lesson is not obvious. In our sales world, "sliding down the obstacle head first" means that sometimes you have to accomplish the selling task by taking a totally different approach to the customer--think outside the box. This is why it's good to talk to people and get input. Someone may show you a different way--headfirst.

Lesson Number Seven: "If you want to change the world, don't back down from the sharks."

We all know who the sharks are--they're our competitors who, sometimes, will do anything to derail the sale we're trying to make. The lesson here is not to back down. Don't become a shark yourself, but aggressiveness in the pursuit of a sale is not a fault. As I have said to my sales folks often: GTO (Get the Order) but don't compromise your principles in the process. That's the game we have to play.

Lesson Number Eight: "If you want to change the world, you must be your very best in your darkest moment." Everyone experiences dark moments. In our world, it's often the loss of a big order that everyone was looking for. It is at this moment that you go into the "debrief" mode that I've written about several times. Understand what got you into this place and make sure you figure out how not to get there again--get help, talk to people, don't go through it alone.

Lesson Number Nine: "If you want to change the world, start singing when you're up to your neck in mud." There's another way to put this: "never let them see you sweat." In our sales world, we have to be optimistic no matter what happens. I like to use the example of a successful baseball player: a successful major league baseball player gets an average of 3 hits for every 10 at bats and may experience 20 or more at bats with no hits. A pitcher may have a horrible inning, but he has to come back and pitch again in the next inning. When you're up to your neck in mud, sing. Try it.

Lesson Number Ten: "If you want to change the world, don't ever, ever ring the bell."

"Ringing a bell" for a SEAL is quitting. A salesperson, like a Navy SEAL, like a baseball player, should never give up. Keep swinging; keep fighting; keep finding new customers and taking care of old customers--just don't ring the bell.

Great Salespeople are Great Leaders

"Some cadets that are really high performing, they just go about their own business," said Colonel Ryan, of the department of behavioral sciences and leadership at West Point. Ryan was speaking about Captain Simone Askew who became the first African American to be named First Captain, leader of the West Point Corps of Cadets. "She is just a leader in every sense of the word, figuring out how she can connect people together and serve others." New York Times, Emily Cochrane, August 14, 2017.

Captain Askew was interviewed on CBS News and asked how she got to the top--against all odds. Her response was that she couldn't get there by herself. She needed help--other people--mentors, colleagues, friends--to get there. Askew said: "Allow yourself to be a vessel. Throughout my cadet career I've just really focused on being poured into, seeking advice, seeking development, leadership mentors wherever I could. Just truly be a vessel and be poured into." Great salespeople need to become vessels, learning from those around us, learning from our customers.

We all make a big mistake when we think we can succeed without help. Really successful salespeople reach out to others to give them insights and intelligence that will overcome the barriers to sales.

And what keeps us from asking for help? Pride. Humility is a key to sales success. Our egos are a huge barriers to success in sales.

Don't be afraid to reach out and ask for help to close that order, or to prepare for that sales presentation. Dare to be great by daring to be humble.

Bring all possible resources to bear when you go after that new prospect or try to close that big sale.

Anatomy of a Lost Order I

If you Google "Peter Drucker" (world famous management consultant and author of many books) you will find hundreds of great quotations. His most famous one was "Doing the right thing is more important than doing the thing right." For purposes of this section, we're going to examine his quotation: "Culture eats strategy for breakfast, technology for lunch, and products for dinner, and soon thereafter, everything else too." Culture is a "top down" thing; it determines the way we look at ourselves and our jobs. Let me give an example. A company that I'm familiar with demands that its salespeople "sell" a minimum of three units a month. The boss doesn't care how it gets done, just that it gets done. You can see how this culture (if you can call it that) eats strategy, technology and products right up. Everything takes a back seat to the sale--to the transaction. (Remember The Transaction Salesperson?)

But, if you know you're competing against a salesperson so desperate to get the order to make a quota that he'll give the product away at very little margin, you know how to beat him. Rebekah Iliff discusses this in the (July 31, 2017 issue of INC magazine.)

Relationships build companies, not transactions. "Making an emotional connection with the buyer is what matters." The culture that we're promoting is a relationship driven culture, not a transaction driven culture.

To beat "Transaction Salesperson" to the order you have to work harder to build a relationship with the customer. You have to understand that all the Transactional Salesperson has to sell is price—They have to get the order. Therefore, you have to find a connection with the buyer that goes beyond price. Iliff's suggestions:

1. **"Make an emotional connection with the customer."** This will demand some homework. Use LinkedIn and Facebook to understand his personality; use Google and Bing to understand his company. Do your homework before making that first sales call. Remember, you have to beat the transactionals salesperson and it better be something other than price that sells your product.

2. **"Understand that the customer has to be comfortable."** You have to demonstrate that you know more about your product and the right solution than your competitor. Don't be afraid to get help in this area. Be humble, ask your col-

leagues for help. And never be overconfident. Customers hate that.

3. **"Set clear expectations and follow them."** Make sure the customer understands that what you're offering transcends price; you're putting yourself and your company into the mix.

4. "Communicate till you're blue in the face." Never, ever say--"this order is in the bag." Be Humble and Assume Nothing. Your culture is relationships, not transactions. Relational culture beats transactional culture.

Product knowledge, humility, relationship building. These are the things that beat someone who is just using pricing to get an order.

Anatomy of a Lost Order II:

I was stunned when I read this LinkedIn post from Joshua Wamser, President of *Industrial Compressor Solutions*: *"During your interview, I was there. You didn't notice me, because I was dressed like a service technician. You walked past myself and another potential coworker 3 times without ever saying hi. You were very cordial to the people you believed to be in charge though. None of us are better than anyone else. Say hi, smile, wave, or engage everyone you can."* This is a classic example of how to lose a sale--of not being aware of your surroundings; of not understanding who your customer is; of not doing basic research before your sales call. So, a salesperson makes a call on Industrial Compressor Solutions and ignores the president and talks to the guys in the polo shirts or suits--thinking that they're the decision makers. Anyone who has been reading this book knows that this has violated several sales rules. If any salesperson walks into a customer's facility without understanding who the players are then he needs to go back to Sales 101. And this goes for any kind of salesperson. Have you ever been in a situation in which there have been two customers together, one male and one female, and the salesperson addresses the male, thinking the female is NOT the decision maker? Underestimating the influence of one or the other person while making a pitch is a sure way to lose the sale. I have a customer who are a wife and husband team and the wife is the president of the company. I can't tell you how many times I have watched sales folks address the husband and ignore the wife--and LOSE the sale. When you're making a sales pitch, make sure you understand who the players are and their roles in the decision making process. If you don't know, ask. Take your blinders off or risk losing the sale--it's that simple. It's very interesting to watch a salespersons eyes: are they on the man who they think is the decision-maker, or treat men and women equally—with their eyes.

Anatomy of a Lost Order III:

Understanding how an order was lost demands brutal honesty--and honest self-examination--something salespeople are often reluctant to expose. The July 8, 2015 issue of The Harvard Business Review did a survey of 230 buyers, asking them to grade the salespeople who come to them to sell their products. The results are shocking: the buyers rated only 12% of salespeople as "excellent;" 23% as "good;" 38% as "average;" and 27% as "poor." There was no corresponding interview of salespeople to ask them how they rated themselves, but I suspect 80% of us think we're "excellent" and 20% think we're "good." Ego is important when you have a job that involves so much rejection, but ego is a deal killer in the buyer's office.

What are buyers looking for?

1. **They want to TRUST the salesperson;** they want to feel that the salesperson is being honest about his product and what it can do--and being honest about what it can't do.
2. **They want a salesperson who can converse intelligently.**
3. **This is huge!** How does a 30 year old salesperson converse intelligently with a 55 year old buyer--one who's heard it all? This demands a well-rounded salesperson: one who reads the newspaper, reads books, knows "stuff"--not just his product. This demands a salesperson who reads about

and understand the customer's business, who looks around the customer's office and sees the customer's interests and can talk about lots of things.

4. **The buyer wants** to understand how the salesperson's product is going to help his company and how the salesperson's company is going to be there to help solve after-market problems.

5. **The buyer doesn't want to feel like he's being forced to order.** I've known lots of salespeople who push the issue--"my kid's going to college, I need the commission. Come on, give me the order." This is not a good strategy. Giving you the order puts the buyer at risk (what if he made a mistake with your product). You have to make him feel comfortable with giving you the order.

6. **Make a personal connection** with the buyer and make sure he understands that you will be there for him if there are any problems with the order.

7. **Be humble. Buyers hate arrogance.** If your product was the best in the world, they wouldn't need salespeople; if your company were the best in the world, they wouldn't need you. You, the salesperson, are simply a channel to get your product into the customer's hands to help him solve a problem. Be the best channel you can be.

TRUST, HONESTY, HUMILITY, COMFORT, CONNEC-
TION--these are the traits that make you "excellent."
When you analyze why you lost that order, you have to ask
yourself if you communicated these traits to the buyer. Ask
honestly and brutally.

Anatomy of a Lost Order IV:
The centerpiece of the World War II movie, "Twelve O'Clock
High," is a debriefing that takes place after a mission. The nav-
igator was three minutes off on his bomb release and missed
the target, and, of course, there was hell to pay at the debriefing.
The consequences of that kind of mistake are enormous--much
greater than losing an order. (Although some bosses may disagree.)

We need to discuss the importance of analyzing the lost sale-
-of understanding how it was lost and how to prevent future losses.
We often just want to forget that we lost that big order; even
more, we don't want anyone to know that we lost it--most of
all our bosses or our colleagues.

Baseball players don't have the luxury of ignoring mistakes.
Their strike outs or errors are shown on the JumboTron for all
to see and criticize. When a salesperson loses an order, it's easy
to hide it--usually--unless you've bragged about getting it before
you actually got it. But, did you ever notice that a major league
batter often heads down to the clubhouse after a bad at bat to

look at the video to analyze what he did wrong. That's what I'm talking about here.

In the military, there is no detail that is too small to be brought up on the debriefing. In the "lost order" category, there is no detail too small to be discussed with your boss or colleagues. You're all in this together and you need to find a solution to the lost order. George Santayana famously said: "Those who don't learn history are doomed to repeat it."

The answers to these questions must be brutally honest:
1. Was the order lost because of price? Really? Orders are rarely lost because of price, so the answer is not the obvious one.
2. Did you lose it because of poor follow up?
3. Did your competitor introduce some features that your product doesn't have?
4. Did your competitor have a better relationship with the customer? Really? Relationships are critical to sales success.
5. Are you sure you were absolutely clear about the capabilities of your product and your company? Did you spend the time to present your company and your products and service capabilities?
6. Have you talked to the customer and asked who won the order and what the reasons that he chose the competitor rather than you--have you "debriefed" the customer?

7. Can you meet with the customer and discuss the reasons that he chose the competition and not you?

8. Often, our attitude is--"okay, I lost it, now let's move on to the next one." Well, you're going to lose the next one if you don't understand how you lost the last one. Don't be afraid to dissect the lost order--even to the point of interviewing the customer who went with the competition. Don't get mad, GET SMART!

How to Get to Carnegie Hall

We sales folks never think that our jobs require practice. Practice is what musicians do; it's what actors do; it's what athletes do-- not what sales people do.

I was speaking recently with my good friend, Sal, a small business owner. Sal is a volunteer firefighter and he was talking with me about how, once a month, firefighters are required to operate every piece of equipment--including doing things as simple as extending ladders. Even firefighters, who have been doing their jobs for decades, are required to go through the practice--no one is excluded.

So what does this have to do with us sales folks? I have spoken over and over again about the need for preparation. NEVER go into a meeting without an agenda. But I'm going to suggest something more. I'm going to suggest that you actually practice your sales pitch. Practice it on your wife; your kids; your boss; your colleagues.

Salespeople who thinks that they're too good or too smart to practice are misleading themselves. When I ride with a regional sales manager or another salesperson, I like to go over the proposed sales pitch--practice it over and over. In fact, one of the regional managers that I rode with used to debate with me: he would take the part of the customer or he would take the part of the competitive product sales person. We were constantly discussing the merits of our product and debating the merits or failings of the competitive products.

Salespeople NEED to practice their craft.

When I have a major sales presentation coming up, I always plan is to have the presenters meet the morning before the meeting and prepare very carefully. I refuse to go into a meeting without thorough preparation--without practicing and without an agenda.

How do we keep robots from taking our jobs? By being better--PRACTICE, PRACTICE, PRACTICE. As I said previously, overconfidence is a deal killer. Practice requires humility; it requires you to admit that you can get better. And every one of us can get better. Be humble; practice your craft.

Over-Confidence: the Mortal Enemy of a Salesperson

"Don't worry, I got this." "Don't worry, this customer is in my pocket." "Sam wouldn't do anything until he checks with me." I cringe when I hear those words from a salesperson. Your customer has one purpose in mind--if he wants to keep his job--to make the best deal for his company. So, while you're out patting yourself on the back because you feel that your customer is in your back pocket, think again.

The cardinal rule of a good salesperson is NEVER to think he has the order in his pocket; NEVER to think the customer will call before they decide to go with the competition. Fear of losing the order is a great trait to have as a salesperson. As long as you fear that you will lose the order, you will stay with it until the check clears.

One thing that customers don't like very much is that constant call asking if they placed the order yet. So there's a thin line between being a pest and being over-confident.

You need to call, but you need to be offering something new when you call. You need to develop a follow up strategy (just like a post-sale strategy) that keeps you communicating with the customer so that your voice is the one that rings in his head (in a good way) when it's time to place the order.

For example, lead time update is always a good reason to call; any product updates is also a good excuse. The point is, have a reason to call both before and after the sale.

Never assume the order.

Oops. What happened? They promised me the order.
Inc. Magazine had a very insightful article recently about a step that is often missed in the sales process. ("The One Sales Step that Most Sales People Miss," by David Finkel, July 21, 2021). You get the order, you go back to your office and celebrate with your colleagues. Next day the customer calls you (if you're lucky) and tells you they gave the order to your competitor or that they decided they didn't need the product after all. This has happened to every salesperson at least once. What happened? They promised you the order.

What could have happened was that your competitor was more involved than you. They got a second look. They went back and back again and made a better deal. You tell your boss that your "greedy" competitor took the order by "dumping the price." And you know that's not what happened. You know they took the order by one-upping you. They were the last in and they could have taken it by just promising better service or by showing the customer they wanted the order more.

When a customer says you have the order, that is NOT the order--a promise to place the order is not the order. My wife, who spent her career in credit and collections, says an order is not an order until the customer's check has cleared. I can't tell you how many times a salesperson has called me and said "I got it--I got the order." And my response is always--you don't have the order. You have a promise of an order. So many things can happen after the customer promises you the order: your competitor one-ups you; your manufacturer can't deliver when the customer wants the order; your customer credit doesn't pass; etc. etc.

The lesson is simple: stay close to your customer all the way from the promise to the delivery to the payment. Then, and only then, can you celebrate.

Finkel suggests a "post sell plan:" Make sure the customer is comfortable with his decision by making them feel good that they made the right decision. Make sure there's no room for buyer's remorse or for testing the market with other suppliers. And make sure the customer knows what the process from now until shipment is.

To quote Finkel: "By strategically and systematically building in a 'post sale' step into your sales process, you'll keep more of the business that you would otherwise have lost through buyer's remorse" and other reasons.

Stay close to your customer until the product is paid for. Then celebrate!

CHAPTER NINE

Collaboration

General Stanley McChrystal, with Chris Russell, has published a book entitled "One Mission." (Pan Macmillan, August 9, 2018) It is a discussion of teams and teamwork and how teams are more effective than individuals because teams bring the power of multiple brains to a task. But we are salespeople, and sales people are loners. We don't want to involve others because that will affect our sales dollars and maybe our commissions--and bosses will think less of us because we can't close without help.

The facts show that success comes from collaboration--so how do we reconcile our need, as salespeople, to go it alone and the fact that we can be more successful if we collaborate in our efforts? Fortunately, technology comes to our rescue here. There are lots of "apps" that allow us to collaborate and still go our ways as independent salespeople.

The hottest new app for collaboration is "Slack" (www.slack. com). Someone described it as a text messaging system on steroids.

Matt Mansfield, in his Small Business Trends blog states: "Integration is what catapults Slack into a category all its own. The solution enables you to centralize all your notifications, from sales to tech support, social media and more, into one searchable place where your team can discuss and take action on each."

So, instead of scrolling through your text messages to find that note that you sent your sales manager, you use Slack to keep track of all messages on all subjects.

Three things that are very very important--Slack is free for small businesses: Slack is very customizable so that you tailor it to your business; and Slack is available for all platforms--smartphones, tablets, laptops and desktops, Android and IOS. Slack is organized by "Channels," so that you can have a separate Channel for different parts of your business, including Private Channels for management, sharing files, and sending notifications to your team--all the stuff that is difficult to do with texting.

Check it out. Collaboration is the secret to future success in sales with the world moving so fast; Slack is a free and easy way to collaborate. Much better than email, and more effective than texting.

Getting Organized--the Old Way:

Back in the 80's, before Facebook, Twitter, email, texting, and cell phones, I used an organizing system called ScanCard. Good old paper and pencil. Notes written on a card and inserted into a "control panel" for easy viewing. The original owner sold the company and computers and cell phones made scan cards too "old style." The system went out of use.

Recently, one of my colleagues reminded me of this system. He was overwhelmed by all his emails, texts, phone calls, sales calls--with no way to organize at the things he had to do for customers. He remembered the card system I used to use. He thought that this would be a good way to organize himself. You can use a note pad, but then you have to find the page you wrote the notes on--you have to remember that you were supposed to do something for someone, you spend a lot of time reading over old pages to find what you're looking for.

So I Googled "ScanCard" and found the system has been revived and was now owned by the original owner's son.

With the ScanCard system, you see it all in a glance: emails that have to be followed up on, texts that need your attention, calls that have to be returned--everything is there to be looked at every day.

Keep the cards by your side making notes as you read your emails, as you watch TV, during customer visits--all your notes go into the binder for easy viewing.

I have stepped back into the 80's and ordered the ScanCard system once again. Sometimes things that are old are better than things that are new. (I speak from personal experience.)

Getting Organized--the New Way:

Everyone has a smartphone these days. And every smartphone has a "Reminder" app. If you have an iPhone ™, make the included "Reminder" app a widget and use it to add reminders and notes. Make sure you make a date for the time the task must be finished and you can add notes to your Reminders and you can even tell the app to remind you of the task when you're texting the person involved in the task.

Android™ and iPhones™ both have a free reminder and note taking apps which I use regularly: Google Keep™. You can set reminders with Google Keep™:

Open the Note that you want to set a reminder for.

Tap the Remind Me icon in the top right corner.

Select or fill out the following sections:
*   Later today

- Tomorrow morning
- Friday morning
- Pick a date & time
- Pick a place

The lesson here is not to depend on your memory, no matter how good you think it is. I say this many times, over and over, in this book:

Keep lists and make them reminders and check them every

Reply to All... DON'T:

Have you ever "Replied to All" and found out your comment went to someone you didn't realize was part of the email chain? And then you had to apologize to that person? Everyone has. Sending emails to multiple recipients is very common.

Some of the emails I receive will have 40 or 50 people in the "To: field."

And if I "Reply to All," then all 40 or 50 people get my comments. And then all hell breaks loose. Email after email, response after response, now barrages your Inbox. "Yeah, great idea," says one. "Right on" says another. None of these responses contributes to anyone's knowledge. The responses are nonsense.

But there is a solution: BCC.

Hidden in your "Compose Email" window, usually over on the right side of the screen, are two links: CC and BCC. You have to click BCC with your mouse to get it front and center in your email composition page.

BCC means "blind copy." This means that the person receiving your email will not see the other people who received your email and if the recipient Replies to All their email will only go back to you and not to everyone else you sent it to. The only names and email addresses the recipient sees are yours and his. If you want recipients to know you sent this to a Group, then state it in the email body: "This email has been sent to all field salespeople." *Don't put all the names in the To: or CC: fields.* And if all your sales staff are in a group called "Field Sales" and you send it to this group in the To: field, everyone is copied in a Reply to All. If you put the Group in the BCC field, problem solved. (So many sales managers list every salesperson in the To: field when sending out emails. Put the list into the BCC field and just state in your email that this is being sent to all field sales staff. Simple, right? If you want to make sure your group list is correct, send the list out every once in a while to have it checked by the recipients. How many group lists contain employees who have left or been fired? Keep your groups clean to prevent competitive information from getting out.)

Use BCC when sending emails to many people and everyone will love you for it. Use BCC when you don't want the recipient to know who else you copied on the email.

Use BCC.

If you want cooperation and comments, don't use email

CHAPTER TEN

So You Think
No One's Watching...

Inc. Magazine published an article entitled "8 Small Things People Use to Judge Your Personality" by Travis Bradberry. (May 18, 2017)

The article hits the nail right on the head. We think no one's watching us--but they are. And they're using our actions to judge whether they're going to do business with us--whether they're going to buy the product we're selling. Remember, you have competition and often the competitor is selling something very similar to your product. So how does the customer tell which one to buy? The customer uses clues; often clues that

THE FINE ART OF SELLING

we're unaware that he's using; often clues that even the customer is unaware of. I know these 8 items are important because I've used them to judge people myself. (Note, the words in quotes are directly from *Inc Magazine*. The comments after the quotes are my own.)

The first one is a real insight into a person's over-all personality:

1. **"How Do You Treat Waiters and Receptionists?"** You're out to lunch with a customer and the waiter brings the wrong meal to you or to your customer. Are you sensitive to the mistake ("everyone makes them") or do you fly off the handle? The receptionist doesn't get your name and you have to repeat it three times. Do you get angry? Your customer is watching--and judging and making his mind up about whether you're going to get his business. Everyone watches how you treat other people and judges you based on how you react. I could expand this to "how do you treat your colleagues, your employees, and others." More than anything, how you treat others in public is a window into your soul.

2. **How Often Do You Check Your Phone?** I have mentioned this often in the book. You think you're being sneaky--looking at your phone on your lap; you think no one's

paying attention--they are and it could lose you the order. It will definitely lose you the respect of the customer or colleague. Put the phone away.

3. **"Repetitive, Nervous Habits."** The best way to approach a sales call is to sit still, listen, take notes and ask questions. Fidgeting with your hair, clicking your pen, glancing at your phone--all bad. Be aware of your nervous habits and get rid of them. Ask people if they notice you have nervous habits.

4. **"How Long Do You Take To Ask Questions?"** This little issue can drive a customer crazy. And this goes to an issue I've mentioned several times: have an agenda and prepare your questions. Taking a long time to ask a question = poor preparation and poor product knowledge. That's the message you're giving to the customer when you hem and haw: I don't know my product and I don't understand your business.

5. **"Your Handshake."** I have already discussed the importance of body language. Standing straight and tall and offering a strong handshake will start the sales call off right.

6. **"Tardiness."** Being early for an appointment shows respect; being late shows lack of respect. We have all had the experience of sitting in a doctor's office and waiting, and waiting, and waiting. The message that I get when that happens is that the doctor has no respect for me or my time. Well, that is the message you are sending when you're late for a sales

call. If you're going to be late for traffic or such, call. Or better, plan ahead so you're early; take account of possible traffic issues.

7. **"Handwriting."** Cursive writing is not even being taught any more so I don't feel that this applies to a sales person.

8. **"Eye Contact."** This relates to item 5 above--body language. Standing straight and tall, offering a firm handshake, making eye contact, turning off your phone--all indicate a person who wants the order. The customer reads eye contact with "truth." It's very difficult to look someone in the eye and not tell the truth.

Examine yourself--honestly--and change the things that need to be changed to make yourself a successful sales person, a successful employee, a successful person.

What Do Winners Do?

In a recent interview with Joe Maddon, Manager of the 2016 World Series Champion Chicago Cubs, and Theo Epstein, then President of the Cubs (now in the Red Sox organization), they pointed to a couple of things that they did differently and that contributed to their success. Most notable, and the thing that really jumped out at me, was that they scouted out their opponents before every game.

Normally, baseball scouts are out looking for new talent. Not

Cubs' scouts. Cubs' scouts were analyzing the next opponent's hitters: what do they swing at? Where is their sweet spot--where do we not pitch? Their strategy was to secure a team of strong hitters and scout the opponents' hitting weaknesses so that their pitchers started with an advantage.

Bill Belichick, former head coach for the Super Bowl champion New England Patriots, had a similar strategy. He had a room full of assistants looking at every single play of their next opponent's previous games, analyzing minute changes in everything, from the angle of the quarterback's head, to the slight movement of the right guard--all to find out the opponent's weaknesses.

I have said over and over again in this book that product knowledge is a critical component of sales success. And that is true. But just as critical is knowledge of your opponent--understand your competitors and their weaknesses and strategies.

What motivates a customer to make a decision in favor of your product can be very subtle. Bill Belichick and Joe Maddon understand that fact. Everyone who wants to be successful in sales must also understand that fact.

Take the time to know who you are competing against; take the time to understand your competitors' product--because taking that time could mean the difference between success and failure, between winning and losing.

THE FINE ART OF SELLING

The "Triple Double"

A "triple-double" happens when a basketball player reaches double digits in three of five skills--usually points, rebounds, blocks, steals and assists--all in the same game. The most common way to achieve a triple-double is through points, rebounds and assists. The most triple-doubles in one NBA season is 42-- by Russell Westbrook.

Why do I bring this athletic feat into a conversation about selling?

Because, in order to accomplish a triple-double, a player needs three essential skills: knowledge of the game, knowledge of his competitor, and passion. And these exact skills are the same required for a good sales person.

In a recent interview with Westbrook, when asked how he manages to achieve so many triple-doubles, he stated that, during the game, his only friend is the basketball. It's all about the ball.

In fact, during the 2017 playoffs, for the first time in NBA playoff history, he got a triple-double in the first half of the game! Remember, a triple-double is not just scoring points; this involves assists and rebounds--it involves teamwork; it involves being in the game at every minute; it involves knowing and understanding the game.

And what is the triple-double for us sales folks? Product

knowledge, customer knowledge, and passion. With all three of these components, we succeed. They are essential components to success:

Know your product and your competitors' product inside and out;

Know your customer and his needs and how you can resolve his issues;

Passion: believe in yourself and your product and company.

CHAPTER ELEVEN

Asking the Right Questions

C an Artificial Intelligence Do My Sales Job???
Everywhere we look today, robots are taking our jobs. Back in 2012, travel agents began to be made obsolete because airlines installed new ticketing systems that allowed travelers to buy tickets online and make their own travel arrangements. In the 1980's there were almost 50,000 travel agents in the U.S. Now that number is less than 15,000.

Cars are being assembled by robots and driven by computers. Where is this all going?

First of all, by "robot," I don't necessarily mean a robot. By "robot", I am referring to general automation of any job, from online ordering to self driving cars to actual walking, talking robots. I am referring to having your job automated in some way--making you obsolete.

So, what exactly is "selling" and how can it be automated and should we sales folks feel threatened?

This is a huge subject with lots of examples of what not to do. Once upon a time there was a huge, big box, computer-selling store called Circuit City. People went to the store, determined what they wanted, and then went home and ordered it online.

And Circuit City went out of business.

The underlying cause of the problem is *Failure To Adapt* to current conditions.

Another example is McDonald's. During the past few years, burger restaurants like Five Guys, and Burger Fi have risen to tremendous popularity because people wanted their burgers fresh and custom. McDonald's had the kitchens, the personnel, the hamburger supply chain, but they failed to adapt and now they are losing their market share to these boutique burger joints.

As Einstein recommended, we should be spending 55 minutes thinking about what our personal strengths (and weaknesses) are and 5 minutes making sure we are playing to those strengths (and eliminate the weaknesses).

Circuit City would be around today (like Best Buy, for example) if they had recognized the trend to online purchasing and made their stores into showrooms and allowed purchase online. McDonald's could have chosen to make some of their stores into boutique, made-to-order burger restaurants.

As salespeople, we have to adapt to future trends. We need to understand automation and how it will impact our jobs and we need to use it to enhance our abilities; we need to be specialists in our products--no matter what that product is, and be the absolute best at what we do.

What is it that automation cannot duplicate? Real product knowledge, the ability to apply that knowledge to the customer's problem, and PASSION for your product.

If you are not committed to your product, to your industry, to your customer--if you are not *passionate*, the computer will win. And do not ignore the benefits of online purchasing. Embrace it. Understand it. And make sure your customer knows that what you give him can't be automated: knowledge of your product,knowledge of your customer's problem and how to solve it, service after the sale, and PASSION.

"Owning" the Agenda

First and foremost, I believe that every single meeting or activity, whether it's a sales call, or a sales meeting, or a board meeting, should have an agenda.

And every agenda should have a "mission" or purpose. And

every item in the agenda should have its own mission or purpose, as well as an expected or proposed solution or outcome. And why such a big deal about the agenda?

The person with the agenda is the person who controls the meeting. If you, as a salesperson, go on a sales call with an agenda and present the agenda to the customer, you "own" the meeting.

And this is true for any meeting. Every meeting should have a mission or purpose and that purpose is the title of the agenda; and every item on the agenda should have a purpose: to achieve the mission.

This is a fact: the person with the agenda OWNS the meeting and taking control of the meeting gives everyone in the room confidence that you know what you're talking about. One warning, however: make sure you anticipate all the issues that your agenda will raise and be able to answer questions related to the agenda.

In summary:

1. Make an agenda for every meeting;
2. Make sure every item on the agenda focuses on the mission of the meeting;
3. Make sure everyone at the meeting has a copy of your agenda--even ahead of time so they know you are in control;

4. Stay focused on the agenda. If the meeting moves away, get back to the items as soon as reasonable;

5. Summarize the meeting before everyone leaves;

6. Send an email summary to everyone in attendance as soon as possible after the meeting ("minutes").

OWN THE AGENDA; OWN THE MEETING; MAKE THE CUSTOMER A BELIEVER.

Focus. Focus. Focus.

112 million people watched the "Catch" by Julian Edelman in Super Bowl 51. It was amazing; and no matter who you were rooting for, it was still amazing—the pass had been tipped, three defenders surrounded Edelman, but he still made the catch.

But what is the lesson that we can learn from this great catch? The lesson is that there is an absolute requirement to focus completely on the task at hand. There is no room in the sales cycle for distraction. The customer deserves your complete 100% attention.

It is easy to get distracted from the task on hand in this age of emails and texts. Your customer deserves your focus, your boss deserves your focus.

And what is the major downside of loss of focus:

1. **Mistakes.** If you're not focused on the project at hand,

you make mistakes. Mistakes are costly.

2. **Opening the door to your competitor.** There is always someone else who is after the same order you're after. Once you lose focus, you give a chance for the other salesperson to get in the door.

Focus won Superbowl 51 for the Patriots. Focus will win the order for you. Get all distractions off the table; turn off things that are taking your attention away from the task at hand. Make the "catch"--focus on the order; focus on the customer. Don't lose sight of the football and don't let the competitors steal the ball away!

Momentary distractions can lose an order

A couple of years ago, there was a psychological study of distraction. They "investigated the effect of short interruptions on performance of a task that required participants to maintain their place in a sequence of steps each with their own performance requirements. Interruptions averaging 4.4 s long tripled the rate of sequence errors on post-interruption trials relative to baseline trials. Interruptions averaging 2.8 s long--about the time to perform a step in the interrupted task--doubled the rate of sequence errors." (Journal of Experimental Psychology, February, 2014)

We are living in an age of constant distraction. We all know (although we don't practice) that a glance down at our phone, or responding to a text while driving, can have fatal consequences. But what does this have to do with a book on sales? I have been preaching about Listening Deeply.

Any distraction can have consequences--can result in a loss of an order. You glance down at your phone--2.8 seconds--and you've lost the string of thought your customer is laying on you.

Many people think they can "multi-task." They're not multi-tasking. They're doing many tasks badly.

If you can't put your phone aside, and put your computer aside, and listen deeply to what your customer is saying, what he is asking, then you're not a good salesperson. It's that simple. If you're in a sales meeting and you feel that you need to answer emails while a product presentation is being made, then you're failing your company and your customer.

The key word is FOCUS--focus on the task at hand and put the things that cause distraction aside.

Give Something, Get Something

The idea of "give something, get something" is a sales technique that is often forgotten.

Sales leads are GOLD. Leads can come in from several sources--some good and some not so good. The absolutely best source of leads is someone you've just sold your product to. And every single salesperson can use this method: Ask your customer if there is someone they know who can use the product you just sold. *Referrals, referrals, referrals in sales is like location, location, location in real estate.*

Happy customers are the best sources of leads. Do NOT be embarrassed to ask. You ask for the order and you ask for a referral--this is a one-two punch that needs to be in every salesperson's bag. It should be automatic.

However, it is very easily forgotten in the excitement of getting the order. The absolute first thought when you get an order should be: "where is the next order coming from?" And the answer is: "from the customer who just gave you the last order." Don't be afraid to ask for a referral. Make it an integral part of thanking the customer: "Thank you for the order. Can you suggest someone else who may be in the market for my product whatever your "product" is?"

Ask.

CHAPTER TWELVE

HUNGER!!!

From millionaire motivator Tony Robbins: *"When people ask what it takes to succeed, the one answer I give them is 'hunger,'"* Robbins says in an interview with Alexandra Middleton. "Hunger is that part of you that says, *'I will not stop. I will not give up,'"* Robbins says.

Robbins is absolutely correct. When I look back on my sales career, the little voice that said, every day, "don't stop," "don't give up" is what kept me on top of my game.

How do you get there--how do you achieve that drive that makes you keep going and doesn't allow you to give up even when the odds are not in your favor?

A true salesperson is not driven by money. A true salesperson is driven by the need to close the sale because of their passionate belief that the customer needs your product. The goal line is the purchase order and every bone and fiber of a good salesperson's body is focused on the goal line--closing the order. Getting that order is no different than sinking a three-pointer at the buzzer or kicking a field goal to win the game. If you have that hunger, then you will succeed. If you don't, then you really need to dig deep inside yourself to find it.

NASA flight director, Gene Kranz, famously stated (in the movie *Apollo 13*) "Failure is not an option."

You need to take that same attitude into your sales life every single day: "don't stop, don't give up, failure is not an option."

Prospecting For New Business

Suggestions from: Mark Hunter, CSP, *"The Sales Hunter."* Mark is the author of High-Profit Prospecting: Powerful Strategies to Find the Best Leads and Drive Breakthrough Sales Results *and* High-Profit Selling: Win the Sale Without Compromising on Price.

Have a dedicated time on your calendar to prospect and don't allow interruptions. This is absolutely essential! The most successful salespeople are those who commit time to prospecting and stick to it. *Saying* you'll start prospecting as soon as you've taken care of everything else is not a strategy – it's an escape tactic to avoid prospecting!

Don't start what you can't finish. Prospecting is about following up. Reaching out to a bunch of people and not following up with repeat contacts is never going to result in any type of success.

Believe 110 percent you can help others. If you don't believe in you, why should anyone else believe in you? Top performing salespeople are successful regardless of what they sell. They know their objective is to help others, and what they sell is merely the means to do that.

Qualify quickly. Nothing is worse than having "prospects" in your pipeline that are taking up your time but never become customers. I'm a firm believer in having a prospecting pipeline that is fast moving, allowing you to spend more time with fewer prospects. Yes, that's the exact opposite of what many sales managers are pushing. We have to think quality, not quantity!

Have a prospecting process and stick to it. My rule is you won't know if your process works unless you've executed it for a period of time that is two times the length of your average buying cycle. For example, if it takes three months to move someone from a lead to a customer, then you need to run your process for at least six months before you'll know if it is working. Too many salespeople give up on their plan far too soon.

Don't rely on social media as your primary means to generate leads. Social media is great, but don't over-rely on it. Use it as *one* of your sources. Social media has a long lead time, and too many salespeople starve to death because they've put too much emphasis into social media, thinking it's all they have to do. Use it to create awareness and confidence. The leads you get are purely a bonus.

Follow up promptly. Sounds simple, but more opportunities are lost due to the failure of the salesperson to follow up fast when leads/prospects give an indication of wanting to move forward. Countless opportunities are lost because the salesperson is afraid they'll be seen as too aggressive. If being aggressive helps me close more deals, sign me up!

Use your phone. Don't fall for the myth, "The phone doesn't work because nobody answers it." Sure, the phone isn't as effective as it used to be, but don't give up on it. The phone allows you to have conversations with leads and prospects, allowing you to qualify them more quickly and ultimately help them far beyond what they initially expected.

Don't rely only on the marketing department for leads. It's always great to have leads supplied, but top performers know they have an obligation to get leads and prospects. Relying on the marketing department is merely an excuse for not taking control of yourself.

Make the prospecting process about the other person. It's not what you sell; it's the outcome you can help the prospect with that will get you the high-value prospects you need. If all you're doing is telling others what you do and what your product features are, you'll be doomed to failure.

Networking and Interacting

I just returned from a national sales meeting and something that jumped out at me regarding the younger breed of sales people was the fact that groups of folks from different divisions and different companies stuck together: ate together, drank together; talked together.

The problem with that is that you never find out what's going on in other parts of the company or the other parts of the world or even another division of the company you work for. The purpose of a sales meeting to network with other divisions and other geographies. Knowledge is power and the knowledge you gain from talking to people from other places or other companies or other parts of the same company is invaluable. And this goes for sales people working within one company--the sales people selling refrigerators need to talk to the tool people or the clothing people in a department store.

Networking is critical to sales success. And that means net-working within your department, within your company, within your division and within your industry.

Get out from your little circle, meet people in your industry and other industries because you can learn a lot if you do. Sales can be a lonely job, but by building a network of people who are not your competitors in your market can be very very valuable. There is more to be learned in the sales job than just your product; you need to see how other people do things and apply them to your area. Talk to people and ask them what they do and how they do it. Never stop learning.

CHAPTER THIRTEEN

First Impressions Matter a LOT

From *Inc. Magazine*: "Science has just discovered exactly how long first impressions linger.... To test the durability of quick first impressions, a team of researchers at Cornell University had 55 volunteers view pictures of a woman they had never met before. In some photos she was smiling, in others she was serious-faced. After viewing the picture the subjects rated her personality for qualities like extraversion and friendliness. Then these same volunteers actually met the woman in real life between one and six months later. ... *The impression of the woman's personality the subjects received from the photograph still heavily colored their face to face conversation.*"

So, what can constitute a bad first impression: not paying attention; having your head buried in your computer or cell phone during the meeting; not smiling; not asking intelligent questions that show your interest in what is being discussed; sitting with a frown on your face and your arms folded.

And what makes a good first impression: smiling; firm handshake; listening deeply to the conversation; asking questions that further the discussion; putting your computer and cell phone away; good posture.

A good first impression is a lasting impression; make your first impression a great one.

Details, Details, Details.

We go through our sales day not really thinking about the details--the little things--about the customer's issues and personality, about his business, about little things in his office that display his personality, etc. Let's take a lesson from Bill Belichick, New England Patriots coach. This is from an article by Kevin Duffy, published on MassLive.com December 16, 2016 (emphasis is mine):

"Its essence: Entry-level coaching assistants are responsible for weekly breakdowns of the upcoming opponent, handed in to Belichick more than a week in advance of the game so he can use them as reference points as he conceives a strategy. Offensive assistants focus on the opponent's defense. Defensive assistants focus on the offense. *Both focus on details so insignificant that you'd think Belichick was playing a prank on these kids.*

Phil Savage, who worked as a coaching assistant in Cleveland under Belichick, remembers logging the direction in which the quarterback turned his head prior to each snap.

Between the identification of scheme and detail, each play could take as long 20 minutes to diagram in full. Each game had 50-70 plays on each side of the ball. Each coaching assistant had three breakdowns per week....

In this job, McDaniels said, 'you learned the most valuable lesson that you keep to this day: everything is important.'"

We love to watch football--without realizing the preparations that these teams make for each game. If we prepared for sales calls the way coaches prepare for games, we'd get every order. *Keep a pad, make notes on what you see in your customer's office or facility--details are important. They are the key to understanding your customer's needs and understanding his needs can get you the order!* We recently got an order for a product because our color scheme fit in with the customer's requirements. You just never know, and if you're not attentive to the details, you could lose the order--even with a better price.

Strategy and Tactics in Selling

From Wikipedia: "A tactic is a conceptual action aiming at the achievement of a goal. This action can be implemented as one or more specific tasks. The term is commonly used in business, protest and military contexts, as well as in chess, sports or other competitive activities.

Strategy is undertaken before the battle. Tactics are implemented during battle. These two concepts must work in tandem, without doing so, one cannot efficiently achieve goals.»

In many ways, sales is, indeed, a battle and your enemies are your competitors. The prize is the order--planting your flag on your customer's desk.

I want to stress strategy in this section. Your strategy is to bring all your forces to bear in order to win the order. And what are these forces?

1. **Product knowledge**. This is the absolute foundation for success in sales. Your customer will see right through you if you don't know your product thoroughly. I can't stress this enough--know every little detail of your product; understand why every component of the product is used and what its function is. Do not go forth into battle until you do.

2. **Knowledge of your competitors' products**. You need to know your competitors, not in order to belittle them, but

in order to address the questions your customer may have regarding those products. Remember, your competitor is the enemy in this war and you need to know and understand your enemy.

3. **Knowledge of your customer.** This is the third leg of the strategy stool. If you don't understand your customer and his needs, then you don't know how to present your product in such a way that you will win the order--win the battle. Understanding your customer is more tactical than strategic.

If you go into battle with knowledge of your product, knowledge of your competitors' product and knowledge of your customer and his needs, then the battle is yours to win!

Strategy is undertaken before the battle. Tactics are implemented during battle. These two concepts must work in tandem, without doing so one cannot efficiently achieve goals.

The Welcome Mat: Getting Customers to Like You

Back in "the day," there was an elderly salesman on our staff. He used to love to tell stories when he went in to see customers--often the same stories over and over again. It got so that, when he got out of his car and the customer saw him coming, they would head out the back door. This is not a recipe for success in sales.

What is the trick to being welcomed when you visit customers:
Always have an agenda--know what you're going to talk about
before you get there, and be prepared with the proper information. OK, that gets you the appointment; what gets
you welcomed back?

1. **Know your customer's interests** and be prepared to talk
about it for a minute or two. (Sports is always a good way to
start.) Or you may want to bring up a good book that you've
just read; or a good movie that you may have seen. These are
conversation openers. But keep it short; respect your customer's
time constraints.

2. **Know your customer's industry**. Understand what's going
on in business news that affects your customer. Have a handle
on personnel changes in the business. LinkedIn is a great source
for this kind of information. Get on LinkedIn and use it.

3. **Bring your customer a lead or an idea** that he can use to
enhance his business.

Make yourself a valued and welcomed vendor; learn the art
of small talk: *whatever your profession, you are in sales.*

Thinking Like a Journalist

Salespeople often think they stand alone in their profession. As
I've stated several times in this book, everyone's a salesperson
and, therefore, we need to look at other professions for inspi-

ration. In this section, we look at journalism.

Journalists are among the bravest information gatherers on the planet. They go to dangerous places and ask difficult questions. What can we learn from this profession?

Ask questions, always and everywhere. Ask your customers why they like or don't like your product and build a list of product assets; ask your customers about your competitors' products. Talk to your competitors--don't be afraid. Just be careful how you ask the questions so that you don't want to appear to be prying. Ask, ask, ask--only by asking can you learn.

Journalists let the answer to one question lead them down a path to further questions--digging deeper into the issue. You need to do the same. Delve deeply into the issue. And listen deeply.

What are you trying to learn? How to sell your product better by knowing what your customers like about your product. How to answer their objections to the issues with your product. And how to understand your competitors' strengths and weaknesses.

Salespeople spend too much time talking and not enough time listening and learning and asking questions. Watch a journalist or TV interviewer next time and learn from their technique.

Back to Basics: When the Thrill is Gone

There are days and weeks and even months in every salesperson's life when we wake up and don't have any idea where we're going today or even in life.

What do you do when that day comes?

When a football team starts to falter, the coaches take the team onto the practice field and they run, over and over again, the fundamentals that made them great: blocking, tackling, running, passing. Over and over again.

And what is the selling equivalent of blocking and tackling? It's talking to the people who have brought you to the level that you've reached. It's talking to the good and loyal customers about their business--getting ideas from the discussion; it's talking to your managers and listening for ideas that they may have.

Do not sit in your office and feel sorry for yourself. Good salespeople are natural talkers--like blocking for a football player. Find your five best and loyal customers and go see them. Listen to them. Let them talk about their businesses and where they see their sales coming from.

Talk to your best customers and Listen Deeply to what they're saying. This is guaranteed to get you out of your funk.

CHAPTER FOURTEEN

"I Hate Salesmen"

How often over the past 40+ years have I heard that statement: "I hate salesmen." My response is always--"what do you do for a living?" The answers range from: "I'm a priest," "I'm a full time mom (or dad)," "I'm an auto mechanic," or "I'm a supervisor (or manager) at XYZ factory (or XYZ store)."

And then I launch into my lecture: "Everyone's in sales, like it or not."

If you're a mom, you're always trying to convince someone (your husband, your kids) that your decisions or ideas or methods are the right ones. When you do that, you're a salesperson. And when you truly believe what you're saying, you're a good salesperson.

The same can be said for a floor manager in a store or factory. Sales is a part of everyone's job--a minister or priest trying to convince people to follow biblical precepts, a cashier in a store trying to convince a customer to sign up for a loyalty card. Sales is everything; salespeople are everywhere. They just don't think they're selling. But the components are there:

Product knowledge (why should I sign up for your loyalty card?)

Firm belief in the value of your product (a waiter who has eaten that special plate and vouches for its wonderfulness.

Personal belief in the value of what you're trying to convince the other person: "you can't get that tattoo, you're only 3 years old."

The problem is that there are people out there who try to convince you about something that you know they don't believe in. They are NOT true salespeople. True salespeople believe in what they're selling. What I called "transactional" salespeople are not true salespeople; they are NOT interested in bringing a product or idea to you that will make you or your life or your company better. They are interested in the commission or achieving a quota.

Relational salespeople are the only true salespeople and when you hear the statement "I hate salesmen," you should challenge it. Sales is a noble profession, and we should be proud that we are part of it.

What does it mean to "sell a song"

We occasionally hear the phrase: "She (or he) really knows how to sell that song." What does that mean?

Any salesperson who understands what it means to really "sell a song" will understand what it means to truly *sell* a refrigerator or grinding tool or insurance policy.

Billy Joel celebrated his 100th month of selling out Madison Square Garden in March of 2024. His performance was as good as it was in the first month, maybe even better. He was 74 years old and performed like a 24 year old. He sold every song for two straight hours. Learn from people like Billy Joel and Alicia Keys.

They teach us what it means to believe so strongly in what you are saying (or singing) that you can convince your audience (or customer) he should buy your product (the song or the refrigerator). A singer who cannot sell their song is boring; when you hear a song that is just being sung and not being sold, you turn it off.

This is the same in sales. If you can't believe in what you're selling, your customer will be bored--will turn you off and you won't make the sale.

If you don't believe in what you're selling, you need to find another product or another profession.

If you do believe in what you're selling--if you believe it will change your customer's life, or his business, or the world, reach into your soul and SELL IT, just like a singer sells a song.

The Winding Path to Sales Success

From a September 9, 2016 article by Neil Irwin:

"How does a person get to be the boss? What does it take for an ambitious young person starting a career to reach upper rungs of the corporate world — the C.E.O.'s office, or other jobs that come with words like 'chief' or 'vice president' on the office door?"

The answer has always included hard work, brains, leadership ability and luck. But in the 21st century, another, less understood attribute seems to be particularly important.

To get a job as a top executive, new evidence shows, it helps greatly to have experience in as many of a business's functional areas as possible. A person who burrows down for years in, say, the finance department stands less of a chance of reaching a top executive job than a corporate finance specialist who has also spent time in, say, marketing. Or engineering. Or both of those, plus others."

We often think, as salespeople, that our jobs start and stop with knowledge of the product that we're selling. That couldn't be further from the truth if you're seeking to become a real sales success story.

A successful salesperson understands all aspects of his customer's business; all aspects of his company's products; and all aspects of his competitor's products.

If you think that you're done once you understand a little bit about your product because you have great sales skills and you think that will carry the day, you are wrong. It may get you an order, or a contract, but it won't get you to the top of your field.

I met a young new car salesperson recently who was developing his capabilities as an entrepreneur by running a small weekend business; who was developing his capabilities in engineering by racing a car he built and repaired; and developing his sales skills in a car dealership. This young man is doing all the right things to get to the top because he doesn't stop work at 5pm, he STARTS work at 5am and never stops.

"Brief" and "De-brief" in the sales process

I was fortunate, recently, to be present at a keynote address given by Maj. "AB" Bourke, fighter pilot and motivational speaker. He stated that he had two concepts to discuss in his speech: 1. "Briefing" and 2. "De-briefing" and to show how these they were essential to achieve peak performance in our jobs. The ideal of the "briefing" is obvious: what is the mission? Everyone involved in a mission needs to know the purpose and intended outcome.

In the military, the de-brief is when all involved in the mission take off their name tags and rank insignia and get together as "equals" to assess the mission and evaluate every component of the process. According to Bourke, the de-brief is the most powerful way to accelerate results. The de-brief is "a sacred learning environment and a path to getting better."

Without these two components (brief and de-brief), peak performance is not achievable.

I asked him how this concept applies to an individual sales person who works alone. His response was that we must create a checklist of outcomes that we want to accomplish for the week and for each meeting during the week. This is the "briefing;" this is the mission. We know we're going to be thrown off track during the week, or during the meeting, be we need to continuously refer to the list to put ourselves back on track. Then, most importantly, at the end of each meeting and at the end of the week, we need to evaluate our performance--the "de-brief." Did we accomplish our overall objectives? If not, why not. Be brutally honest with yourself.

How essential is this? Bourke gave an example of the Blue Angels flying group. At the end of an air show, the pilots land and walk from their planes. The crowds want autographs; want to touch them and talk to them. But the pilots all head to a quiet room for the de-brief. It is never, never skipped.

Sales people who aspire to peak performance should never skip the brief and the de-brief; should always have a "mission" for the week and for each meeting and then evaluate the success of the mission with an honest de-briefing.

Sales Lessons from the Olympics

Watching the Olympics, we see these incredible performances by athletes like Katie Ledecky, Simone Biles, Michael Phelps (of course), and so many others--and say "Wow!" Then we get up the next morning and go about our mundane jobs of selling insurance, or refrigerators, or air compressors, or houses, or whatever. "What do they have that I don't have"? you may ask. They are human beings just like us, born with bodies just like ours; some have overcome great physical, mental, or environ-mental obstacles--just like us. What is it, then?

"Inc." magazine's Jeff Haden did a write up on Katie Ledecky and the psychology of success. (Inc Magazine, August 11, 2016

How do Katie, and other Olympians, do it?

1. **They work very, very hard.** "You can't be great at any-thing--unless you put in an incredible amount of focused effort." Katie swims 6,000 yards in the morning and 7,000 yards in the afternoon. Every morning and every afternoon. Not just when she feels like it. "There are no shortcuts." You

have to work harder and longer hours than everyone else and that's the simple fact.

2. **They put in the time.** Jeff Haden: "Every extremely successful entrepreneur ... works more hours than the average person -- a lot more. They have long lists of things they want to get done. So they have to put in the time." If you think you can be successful working 9 to 5, it ain't happening. When everyone else goes home, you need to keep going--learning, growing, searching for new customers. One of the best salespeople I know told me the other day--"when I'm feeling really good about myself, I make cold calls because I know I can deal with rejection then." He just keeps working--there's no way to be successful without continuous, hard work and long hours.

3. **Set hard goals--not easy ones.** Ledecky's goal was Olympic gold. Wow! How about setting a goal to get that customer that you never thought you could get? Make a plan and work that plan step by step. As Haden says, "Never start small where goals are concerned. You'll make better decisions--and find it much easier to work a lot harder --when your ultimate goal is ultimate success." ... When your ultimate goal is that impossible customer.

4. **And never stop.** "Ledecky won gold medals at the London Olympics and then set her sites on Rio." Successful sales-

people never stop establishing goals and then working harder than anyone else to achieve them.

Today will be better than yesterday

The first thought of many successful CEOs at the beginning of every day is:"I will work today to be better than yesterday." This underpins everything and needs to be our daily mantra. Emile Coue', a French philosopher who lived a Century ago, was a proponent of "auto-suggestion"--using your own mind to convince yourself how good and important you are. He started every day with the thought: "every day in every way I'm getting better and better."

Good posture gives you confidence--posing like a super hero makes you feel like a super hero. Well, constantly talking in positive terms to yourself--"auto-suggestion"--and telling yourself that you are good and you are smart and you can do good is just as important as good posture. All of these components go to making up a good salesperson and a good sales call. Any successful professional sports figure has to have two essential components: positive mental attitude and excellent physical capabilities. Mental attitude is critical to success in sales. Start your day:

Every Day in Every Way I'm Getting Better and Better; and I Will Work Today to be Better Than Yesterday.

Scales....Yes, Scales

My hobby is music. I play a couple of instruments (piano, bass, ukulele) and the thing I hate most about learning music is learning scales. Scales are patterns of notes based on a "root" note. The foundation of music is the "scale." The foundation of any song is the scale. Learning scales on an instrument involves learning finger patterns that are unique to the instrument and that produce the sound that makes the music beautiful.

I went to a concert recently ("Dead and Company"--the re-made "Grateful Dead" group) and was amazed by the performance of the 38 year old lead guitarist (I mention his age because the six member group's accumulative age was 485 years). The camera closeups showed his fingers dancing over the guitar fretboard--seemingly randomly. But NO! He was playing scales as fast as a human being could in a pattern that created a wonderful musical sound. The foundation of this music was scales. And he would do these solos night after night in town after town--and they would sound fresh and exciting every time. Just like a great actor in a play running on Broadway year after year.

What does this have to do with the fine art of selling?

We are all musicians; we are all actors. We need to learn our scales or our lines (product knowledge) so intimately that we can perform them day after day. We need to love what we do so much that the performing of these "scales" sounds fresh every time we solo. Our fingers need to dance over the fretboard so well that the customer's only possible decision is to buy our product.

We, salespeople, often sell our profession short. Done properly, the sales job is just as wonderful as the rock musician's job, or the Broadway actor's job.

A story I told earlier in the book regarding a minister who asked what I do for a living. I said that I was a salesman. He responded "I guess someone has to do it." I wanted to say (but didn't out of respect for him) "Mr. Minister, you are a salesman. Every Sunday you are selling." And everyone, at some point in their lives, are salespeople: applying for a job, convincing your kids to do something, etc. etc.

Selling is a great profession. Be proud of it. Be good at it. Be the best at it. Practice it like the musician practices his scales.

Just Driving Around...

When I was in business school in the 60's, there was a management concept promoted by Tom Peters called "Management by Walking Around" (MBWA). The idea was that a good business manager does not sit in an office and manage by looking at spreadsheets. A good manager walks around his shop and talks to his people and listens.

But how does this apply to the sales process? When I started selling, my father was my mentor and he used to tell me--"if you really want to know your territory, don't take the highways--take the side roads; drive through the towns; see what's happening on the ground."

Sales people tend to drive to the customer's location and then drive to the next appointment and the next and then drive home, all on the highways. "Avoid local roads if at all possible; I'm just too busy to take the time."

And how many times have I been in a retail store and watched the sales people congregate and gossip while I flounder about looking for something?

Just as a good manager finds out what's going on in his shop by walking around, we all need to find out what's going on by looking around, walking around, driving around, talking to people. Spreadsheets are one dimensional. Don't stand still waiting for someone to come to you--go out and talk to people and look around and Just Drive Around...

There's so much out there to see and learn if we just get out of our cars and offices and shells.

Doing What Comes Naturally

Everyone has something they do really well. You may not have found this "thing" yet, but there IS something you do well. This theory works the same in sales. Our company sells tanks and air compressors. We once hired a salesperson who had spent his sales career selling tires. After several months trying to sell tanks, he went back to what he was comfortable with: tires. If you ever notice the sales people in a musical instrument store--for the most part, they're musicians. They're comfortable with musical instruments and music, and they often make good musical instrument sales people.

I consider product knowledge the most important ingredient for a sales person. Therefore, you're going to be good at selling something you want to learn about, something you love. I am a manufacturers' representative, so I sell multiple products. I love learning about anything and everything, so this profession worked for me--it was natural.

If you love your product and you love the people who buy your product, you'll succeed in sales.

This rule applies to every type of sales person--from the minister on the altar, to the retail salesperson selling a washing machine, to a mother in a day care center. I know someone who struggled finding herself until she became a mother--and then she became the best mother because she loved being a mother. Is she a sales person? Yes indeed. She works in day care and mothers entrust their children to her because she exudes "motherness."

Sales is something that's in your soul: love what you

do and do what you love and you can be the best sales person on the planet.

Listening Deeply

I attended three meetings recently, one was a teleconference and two were two-day meetings in a conference room with ten people at each meeting.

One thing jumped out at me--there was a very high percentage of attendees who were NOT listening. You might wonder how I could tell on the teleconference when I couldn't see anyone.

Two ways:

1. **Participation:** (If you're listening and mentally participating, you have to have questions. It's just the nature of things. Questions asked means that you're listening deeply.)

2. **Involvement:** (When the organizer asks for comments and only one or two comment, one can assume that the rest aren't listening.)

During the sales meetings at which everyone was present, out of ten people at each meeting, only five were listening deeply. The other five were sitting in the last row, doing emails on their computers. The thing about opening computers at a meeting, the organizer may think that you're participating and using your computer to make notes, so you think you can get away with it. Or the organizer may not want to make a scene. But how disrespectful is this!

Back in the "day," before computers, when I started in sales, there were no cell phones or computers. Customers waited for their quotes or their call backs. Now, every salesperson feels that every customer needs an immediate response. And what is the result of this "immediacy"? Everyone loses. The group loses the possibly important comments of the distracted participants and the distracted participants lose by not learning the content of the meeting.

This distracted "attendance" has to stop. Computers and cell phones have to be shut off. We need to LISTEN DEEPLY and participate. Do the quote later. The world will not come to an end if the quote is done later or if the call is not returned immediately.

Think about the financial investment that the organizer has in the meeting. When you're not involved, when you're not listening, you are wasting the organizer's money.

Show respect: to the meeting organizer and to the other participants. Listen Deeply and participate!!!

Product Knowledge
I have mentioned the importance of product knowledge several times. In fact, , I put product knowledge at the top of the list

of necessary attributes for a successful salesperson.

A customer that I'm familiar with lost an order for an air compressor recently because he said "the end user wanted rigid pipe connections on his compressor rather than flexible hose." Our compressor had flexible hose and the salesperson did NOT have enough product knowledge to overcome the objection. Our lives are surrounded by flexible hose of all types. There are thousands of flexible hose connections in a jet engine; tens of thousands of flex hoses in a Apollo rocket. Flexible hoses (usually a corrosion resistant interior liner surrounded by wound stainless steel braiding) are everywhere--look under your toilet at the connection to the water inlet.

Why are flex hoses so prevalent? Two reasons: They're easier to install than rigid. And because they can absorb shock and vibration better than rigid pipe--flex absorbs, rigid pipe cracks. We all know that rocket engines and jet engines vibrate, sometimes rather dramatically, so flex is a natural solution.

But air compressors vibrate and therefore, flex hose is a better option than rigid pipe.

Customers may want a particular configuration on a product you sell. That configuration may not be an appropriate one. The salesperson's job is to explain the issues to the customer, to explain why his product is better than the competitor's. In my mind, a salesperson without product knowledge is not a true salesperson, like a minister who doesn't know the Bible.

An order taker is "transactional:" take the order, give the customer what he asks for, and don't try to educate the customer on why he may be wrong.

Take the time to understand your product. Take the time to understand your competitor's product. Understand why your manufacturer's design may be different and use that difference to sell your product. Don't be an "order taker." Learn your product, right down to the little components that make your product different and better.

Linkedin.com as a sales tool

Linkedin often gets a bad rap as a resource. I've had two conversations recently about Linkedin which were 180 degrees apart. One VP of Sales for a large national company has found out how to use it to find potential customers. Another, the president of a rep agency, was concerned about the privacy since anyone could see your connections and who were looking at you.

Both are corrrect, but the privacy complaint is fixable. Just like Facebook, you can go into your profile and settings and set the privacy settings so that the people who may be connected to you or who may be viewing you are invisible to the rest of the world.

So, if you want people to see you, leave the privacy settings at the default. If you want privacy, change your profile settings to allow privacy.

The next decision to make is whether to go "Premium" or not. Before making that decision, let's look at ways to use Linkedin as a sales tool.

First, if you're on Linkedin and your profile is up to date, then you've basically opened the door to allow people to contact you.

Since finding the decision maker is a critical component of a successful sales strategy, Linkedin is the absolutely best tool for that.

The Long Tail Theory

The concept of the Long Tail was developed in 2004 by Chris Anderson, Editor-in-Chief of Wired magazine. The two components of the tail are: "hits" and "niches." The theory of the Long Tail is that our culture and economy is increasingly shifting away from a focus on a relatively small number of "hits" (mainstream products and markets) at the head of the demand curve and toward a huge number of niches in the tail.

What does that mean to the sales process? I have discussed my ideas with Chris Anderson, and he agrees--a salesperson needs a "hit" to get into the door, but he needs "niches" to really make sales and money. When you call on a customer, there is what Anderson calls "latent demand" and you don't know what it is unless you ask.

Start your sales call with the reason that you're there (your "hit"), but understand that the customer needs other things that you offer and unless he knows what these other things are, he may not know that he needs them.

Once Amazon developed their book selling system, adding an infinite number of products became possible and every new product added revenue without adding significant cost. The same with iTunes and Google.

So let's put this theory into practice:

You go into a auto dealership to buy a car (the hit). A good car salesperson pitches the navigation system, the satellite radio, the moon roof (niches). These are the high profit items for the dealership. An air compressor salesperson pitches the air compressor to the interested customer (the hit) but also pitches the receiver tank, the dryer, and all the fittings and regulators (the niches).

The manager or owner of a store or sales agency or distributorship realizes that the long tail theory means that adding products to the salesperson's offerings works to everyone's benefit as long as the products will be purchased by the same person, or same company. The expense of the call has been covered with the "hit," the money can be made with the "niches"—everything else that the salesperson can sell during the same call.

Amazon got people to go their website by selling books. Now, while someone is buying a book, he can buy anything else he can think of—almost unlimited. While someone is going to iTunes to buy an Adele album, he can buy another other piece of music he may think he wants even if no one else is interested—almost unlimited--because the additional of additional songs adds insignificant cost to Apple.

Their secret is now our secret. Make the tail long and make the sale profitable.

I was at a Van Heusen store recently and bought a pair of slacks (the "hit"), a couple of polo shirts, and some socks (the "niches"). The cashier asked whether I needed a belt. I asked him why he asked and he said: "you seem to have everything that goes with an outfit but the belt and thought I'd ask." So then I asked him where his salesmanship came from. He said that his grandfather, a sales rep for a chemical company, used to take him on sales calls. Sales was in his genes. I ended up buying one more "niche" I had forgotten.

Sitting by the phone, waiting for the order.

You made your pitch. Now you're sitting by the phone waiting for the call from the customer. Waiting to get the order. I have one word for you:

DON'T.

You need to stay in touch with the customer who is in the process of making a decision. You need to email him, call him, call on him in person, anything to let him know that you want the order. Some of the approaches could be: "here's some information I forgot to give you the last time," or "here's an update on the product," "if you're still having a difficulty making this decision, can I see you so that we can discuss your questions?." Use any reason you can think of to stay in touch with the customer during the decision making process.

MAXWELL'S LAW: THE LAST SALES PERSON STANDING GETS THE ORDER.

I play in a big band orchestra and the conductor at a recent rehearsal made a great point: what the audience remembers is your last song. You can mess up in the middle of the concert, but make the last song perfect and that's what they'll remember. Be the last person the customer remembers and you'll greatly improve your chance of getting the order.

Passion, Enthusiasm, Confidence

A new vacuum cleaner salesman knocked on the door on the first house of the street. A tall lady answered the door. Before she could speak, the enthusiastic salesman barged into the living room and opened a big black plastic bag and poured all the cow droppings onto the carpet.

"Madam, if I could not clean this up with the use of this new powerful vacuum cleaner, I will EAT all this cow poop!" exclaimed the eager salesman.

"Do you need chili sauce or ketchup with that?" asked the lady. The bewildered salesman asked, "Why, madam?"

"There's no electricity in the house..." said the lady.

There is nothing that beats being passionate about what you're selling and feeling confident in your product. But how can you be passionate about a refrigerator, a vacuum cleaner or an air compressor?

Passion and enthusiasm come when you're confident, when you know your product inside and out and when you truly believe that your product can solve your customer's problem. This all starts with product knowledge and product belief. Whether you're selling cars, refrigerators, air compressors, lights or religion--whatever, you need to know everything about your product and why it's better than anyone else's. If you don't believe in your product, your customer will see this and you will not make the sale. Although his approach may have been a little over the top, the vacuum cleaner salesman in the joke believed in his product.

Without passion, enthusiasm and confidence, sales becomes a tough job and not a joy.

R-E-S-P-E-C-T

Aretha Franklin made these letters famous in her song of the same name

Several years ago, I was working a trade show booth, helping a business owner by representing my product. During a lull in the trade show action he confided in me that he really didn't "like" his customers. He felt that he was too well educated--"better" than his customers--after all, he owned a business, was college educated, etc., etc. . I thought to myself, during this discussion, this guy's not going to be in business in five years. I way overestimated; he closed his business a year later. He thought he was smarter than his customers. He wasn't. A good salesperson has to RESPECT his customers. If you don't respect your customers--respect them for what they have achieved, for their own capabilities, for who they are, you won't sell them anything.

From the moment you come into contact with a customer, that customer is evaluating you, testing you. If you think you're the smartest person in the room, the customer will sense this lack of respect and your chances of getting the order is reduced geometrically.

If you can't respect your customers, you are in the wrong business. If you can look at a customer and realize--really realize--the value in this customer as person, then you will be successful as a salesperson. Product knowledge is important; but respecting your customers is absolutely essential to your success in sales.

Muscle Memory in sales

One of the joys of my life is playing double bass in a big band. Some of the music we play is at a very high speed. I have to 1. read the notes; 2. have my left hand play the notes at the proper position on the neck; and 3. have my right hand pluck the proper string to have that note make a sound. All at two to three times the speed of a heart beat. You just can't do this if you have to think about what you're doing.

In sales, muscle memory is just as critical as in performing music. When you're in a situation with an aggressive customer who has given you a couple of minutes of their precious time, you had better be able to present your case without stumbling- -just like a musician performing before an audience. A standard question and answer among musicians is: "what are the three things a musician must do to get to Carnegie Hall?

Practice, practice, practice."

In sales, being able to state the best qualities of your product in a couple of sentences, without hesitation and with conviction, is critical to success.

1. **Step 1:** ask the smartest people you know to give you the 5 sentences you need to memorize that describes the best attributes of the product you're selling.
2. **Step 2:** memorize these 5 sentences until you don't have to think about them.
3. **Step 3:** be able to expand on each of these 5 sentences. Have these sentences so deeply ingrained in your brain that they are automatic.

And, if you're selling more than one product, you need to repeat this process for each product.

I can't emphasize enough the importance of this process.

"Always On:" key to success in sales

I was talking to the owner of a landscape company who was replacing the trees at a location. He was asking me--"who makes the decisions at this location. I want to do the mowing. I'm very reliable and can promise a great job. Just introduce me to the decision maker." He didn't know who I was or what I could do. But he was "always on," always selling.

A good sales person is always selling, primarily because you don't know where your next sale is coming from. A good salesperson combines the "referral" with the "always on" concept. Talk about your product with anyone who will listen and see where it goes.

Sales is not a job. It is a lifestyle. It is a career. Being always on and always selling is the lifestyle. The important thing to remember is, when you're always on, you need to be very informative about your products, rather than direct. You're letting people know what you do; what you sell. Let them take you further; let them think they're helping you by referring you to someone who needs your product.

The Perfect Salesperson: a blend

We've talked about the three types of sales person: the relational sales person; the route salesperson (or "order taker") and the transactional sales person ("get the order at any cost"). The perfect sales person is able to blend all three types into one.

I have a plaque on my desk that stated: "It All Starts With The Sale." The sale triggers everything; the sale creates jobs; the sale supports manufacturing, engineering, invention--everything. The sales job is critical to our economy. A relationship sales person creates a feeling of trust; the route sales person creates a feeling of stability; the transactional sales person creates a feeling of urgency. Trust, stability and urgency are the three legs supporting the sales process. The seat of the stool is a joyful attitude that what you are doing is important.

The customer wants to believe you, wants to know that you'll be there for the duration, and that you really want the order--

"I HATE SALESMEN"

you still have to ask for the order. Can't get away from that.

That salesperson has "attitude"

I was discussing my book today with someone I consider in the category of "excellent" in the sales profession. Our conversation revolved around attitude, but not in the negative sense of "he's got attitude," but in the positive sense of someone who loves what he's doing, who loves to be alive, who loves to meet people and help them out, who is cheerful and confident.

Give me a person with a good and cheerful attitude, who is happy selling stuff, and I'll teach him the product and show him where to go to sell it. You can teach product, but you can't teach attitude. And selling, like many professions, involves rejection. Dealing with rejection with a positive attitude, an attitude that says "I'll keep coming back until he gives me an order," is the essence of success in sales.

Give me someone who says--"I love to meet people and get to know people and to understand their business," give that person product training and you have an unbeatable combination. Hire a person with a dour attitude and even with an engineer's knowledge of your product and he will fail as a sales person.

CHAPTER FIFTEEN

Rules for a Successful Sales Career

The First Rule of Sales is: Keep a List and Take Notes. Note-taking is an absolutely essential tool for enhancing learning, productivity, and creativity. It's a simple yet effective way to capture and organize information, which can be beneficial in various settings, from academic to professional environments. Whether you prefer digital tools or the traditional pen and paper, developing good note-taking habits can have a lasting positive impact on your ability to process and utilize information.

Why, you ask?

It enhances memory retention and promotes active listening.

It organizes your thoughts and facilitates review of what happened at the meeting.

It shows the customer that you care about what they say.

It allows you to create a follow up procedure and to make sure that you give the customer what they want, not what you think they want.

Most importantly, you can capture nuances that may be important for following up. A customer's office may offer important clues regarding their interests and hobbies. The notes you take will help you remember these important facts.

A recent article in the New Yorker magazine by Atul Gawande, a surgeon and philosopher who wrote "*The Checklist Manifesto: How to get things right*," (Metropolitan Books, January 2011) discussed the necessity of check lists in certain, if not all professions. The most obvious profession that uses check lists is airline pilots. There are so many details for a pilot to be aware of that a check list is the only way to be certain that you've done everything. The consequences of missing something are quite severe.

The other profession in need of check lists, but who have not yet adopted it universally, is the medical profession. (Did I leave the sponge in, or take it out?) Those hospitals that have adopted check lists have had infections reduced more than 80%! So why not use check lists in sales? Or in the service business? A check list could be a list of your 10 most important customers--a list you look at every day, asking yourself if you've done everything you can to get and keep their business. A check list could be of list of the most important features of your product--did you discuss each of these features with the customer?

Do not depend on memory. Do not depend on habit. Depending on your memory can kill airline passengers, kill patients, and kill sales. Make a check list and check off the box as you complete the item. Whatever your profession.

There is one tried and true way to reduce stress: lists. At the end of the work day, make a list of what you want to accomplish tomorrow. Review the list throughout the day. Psychologists have proven that lists reduce stress. The danger with lists of things to do is that they become too long. The list should be what absolutely has to get done that day. Five items is great; ten items is the maximum.

When a salesperson is making a call on a customer, the effective salesperson makes a list of the customer's needs. The salesperson listens before talking. Asks questions, and makes a list. What does he need to do to get this customer's business? Always listening; always asking questions; always making notes to turn into a to-do list.

What is a salesperson NEVER doing in the presence of a customer? Looking at his cellphone. If there is a mortal sin of sales, it is that. Pay absolute attention to the customer and his needs; make a list of what you need to do to capture this customer's business; and then DO IT. Just do it.

The Second Rule of Sales: No Jokes

Thou shalt never assume that you know your customer's political orientation or tolerance of jokes. It's become commonplace to forward jokes and political comment to a group of people on your email list. I have one word to those reading this:

DON'T

Unless you want your customers to start ignoring your emails. Resist the urge to forward anything not related to the business. I was meeting with a customer several years ago with one of my employees. The customer turned to the employee and said: "Stop sending me those ridiculous emails." I was embarrassed beyond words.

Your customer may not agree with your views and putting them on the spot like this is not a good idea. This goes with your colleagues as well. Resist this urge. What's funny to you may be offensive to others.

The Third Rule of Sales: Keep your promises

My good friend, Leo, sent me a suggestion which I feel is worthy of being one of the rules:

Thou shalt not rest until all of your promises are kept.

How many promises are made by sales people that are not followed up on? A customer asks you for a sample or for some literature and you forget; or you ask someone else to follow through--and it doesn't get done.

Even if you tell someone else to get something done, it's your promise to follow through on.

Simply handing off the promise does not get you off the hook. Follow through until the customer is happy.

I was working, some time ago, with a regional manager of a manufacturer we represented. He wrote stuff down as the customer complained (rightfully) about certain issues with his product. But he never followed up—despite being badgered by me. He just wasted everyone's time and lost credibility with the customer.

Keep your promises.

Fourth Rule: Thou Shalt Never Give Up

The National Sales Executive Association, in 2014, published the following statistics:

- 48% of sales people never follow up with a prospect;
- 25% of sales people make a second contact and stop.
- 12% of sales people only make three contacts and stop.
- 10% or less of sales people make more than three contacts.

- 2% of sales are made on the first contact.
- 3% of sales are made on the second contact.
- 5% of sales are made on the third contact.
- 10% of sales are made on the fourth contact.
- 80% of sales are made on the fifth to twelfth contact.

Never give up because if you do, you join the majority of poor salespeople.

The Fifth Rule: Don't stop till you get to the top

Never give up on a sale until the top decision maker in the customer's company says no. And when the customer gives you a seemingly insurmountable obstacle to getting the order, don't stop until the decision maker in your company says no.
In my experience, sales people give up on the sale too easily.

Don't give up. Keep going until everyone who matters has said "no."

This is a very difficult rule to keep. "My sales manager says that we can't meet the customer's demands for delivery or price." "My regional manager says we can't meet the customer's specifications." The customer says the boss says we're too expensive. Too often we stop here.

There are ways to get to the top people in your quest for the order. Ask for a meeting with your regional manager and their boss. Get your boss involved with a meeting with your customer's boss. Get advice. If the order is important enough, we must keep turning stones over until there are no stones left.

We had a potential for a large order recently, but we needed a referral. We just couldn't seem to find one. There was one company who owned the product but hadn't been very cooperative. So I called them ("called"!). It turned out that the uncooperative boss has left and a very cooperative person had taken their place. He said he'd be glad to provide a referral and we got the big order.

Don't stop till you get to the top.

The Sixth Rule: Make Email your last resort

One thing that a lot of salespeople do is to write long emails--in paragraphs. And the customer has to ferret through the email to find out what the customer actually wants.

Make your emails bullet points, or numbered. That way the responder can respond to each item easily and can use your email as a to-do list.

You need to appreciate the fact that people are getting dozens (if not hundreds) of emails a day. If you want yours responded to, make it easy for the recipient to respond.

Short sentences; bullet points; easy to answer. And to the point!

We have become a society that wants to resolve everything with an email. I was working with one of our sales people the other day and he was trying to resolve a problem. He said the person he needed to get in touch with was not responding to his emails. "Call him," I said.

I believe that the proper order in working with customers and potential customers is:

1. **Face to face.** Nothing beats face to face. I mentioned earlier in the book that a lawyer once told me that he didn't like conference calls because you don't get "the smell of the room." How true that is. You can't understand a customer's needs unless you spend time at his facility and understand who you're dealing with. If at all possible, meet your customers face to face.

2. **Phone** is the second best. Why? Because you get the feel of your customer's voice. Is he upset? Anxious? Mad? I can't tell you the number of times that a customer comes across as upset and angry in emails, but calm when you talk to him. Can't meet face to face? Call!

3. **Email** is the absolute court of last resort. All of us are guilty of saying things in email that we would never say face to face or on the phone. If a customer needs a quote at 11pm, yes, use email. Otherwise, call or, better, visit.

Companies like Amazon and Google think face to face selling is dead. I don't see it. There is nothing like looking a person in the eye to see what he's thinking.

But if you must...

Managing Emails by making a checklist

Email is the most difficult thing to manage in our day. It makes it doubly difficult if we're on the road selling. Responding to an email doesn't end it, despite what we often think. For a real salesperson, the response to the email is only the beginning. Remember, the person you're responding to has as much, or more, on his plate than you do.

What is the answer to email madness? Checklists.

You must assume your email response will not be looked at by the customer. All sent emails that are looking for a response back should go onto your checklist.

A non-response from a potential customer should not be followed up by another email. It should be followed up by a call. Don't let a potential order die because the customer didn't reply to your email. Assume it got caught up in the system. Call him!

Every day, go through your emails and pull out those that need follow up and write them down in a checklist and check them off as you do them. Making checklists requires focus and focus creates orders.

The Seventh Rule: Know your Product

One of the products that I sell is a very complex product. It involves management of the compressed air distribution in a manufacturing plant. The name of the product is ConservAir. I don't believe you can really sell a product that you don't understand, so I spent hours trying to understand this product. What does it do? How is it made? What makes it better than other similar products?

And then, most importantly, how do I make a complex product understandable to the customer. If you don't understand something, you can't explain it. It's that simple.

Can you make your explanation simple enough for your spouse, your kids, your parents? That's the real test of product knowledge.

To explain how ConservAir manages compresses air, I used an analogy, comparing the distribution of air to water:

Imagine a large 2" water hose gushing large amounts of water. Now imagine that you want to water a tree in one part of your yard, some flowers in another part, and you want to power wash your house. So you divide the flow up. And when you want to stop watering the tree, you turn the valve off and the system automatically regulates the flow to the flowers and power washer. It can do this very quickly because of the flow is divided. Each part of the system requiring water can be regulated quickly because the flow is divided up and you're not dealing with the full flow through a 2" water hose. That's what ConservAir does for air flow in a manufacturing plant.

You can tell your customer that you're saving him money, but if you can't tell him how you'll never get the order.

For true product knowledge, you must be able to explain your product in terms understandable to anyone.

I can't emphasize enough that what sets one salesperson set apart from another is product knowledge. When the salesperson knows his product, the sales experience for both the customer and the salesperson becomes a joyful experience. Customers always have different experiences and different educations and bring these experiences and education to the buying event. A good salesperson has to be equal to the task. A customer who has engineering education will have different questions than a customer who is a lawyer, or one whose background is mechanical. If you really know your product, you don't have to worry about the customer's education. You can handle anything.

So, how do you get this "product knowledge" you need to be successful?

I always start with a search engine like Google or Bing. There is tremendous information in cyberspace.

Let's stick with our previous example, Sub-Zero refrigerator.

Just Google: "What makes Sub-Zero the best refrigerator?" We find out, among other things, that Sub-Zero has an interior air scrubber that removes gases emitted by the food.

Wow. Stand back. I'll sell Sub-Zeros every day with that information. And I have just started.

What about the insulation? How much money will that save me every year?

What about the dual compressors and dual evaporators? What advantage is that?

So much to learn to become a great salesperson.

The Eighth Rule: Get inside your customer's head

The reason I titled this book "The Fine Art of Selling" is because selling is an art. Understanding the complex motivations of customers is not an easy task. You have to be very sensitive to what the customer wants and by "customer," I mean everyone involved in the purchase decision. You may be talking about your product with one person, but there may be many involved in the decision process. A good salesperson needs to find out how the decision is being made.

A salesperson makes money by selling stuff. A good salesperson spends time understanding his customer and the decision making process. A bad salesperson just tries to sell stuff, and if they meet resistance, quits and walks away.

I had a situation recently where a customer called me and asked for a quote on a particular item--and gave me the model number. I could have quoted him and gone on my way. But this is not my style and not what made me successful. I asked questions, and more questions; and my questions lead to other questions and I found out the situation was NOT what I thought it was. Just quoting him, and maybe getting the order and making $25 commission, is what a bad salesperson does. Asking questions and turning one possible order into a situation where you now own the customer because you took the time to understand what he really wanted will turn him into a huge customer and many hundreds of dollars in commission.

Spend the time to get into your customer's head.

Own your customer.

Understanding the customer's "motivation to purchase" is key to making the sale. In a manufacturing facility, the purchasing agent is motivated completely differently than the plant manager and both are motivated differently than the owner. A woman with 4 kids is motivated differently than a grandmother. This may seem obvious--but it's most often not considered by the salesperson in his presentation.

If you're bringing a new product to a purchasing agent, you need to understand that his bosses are evaluating him based on quality, price and on-time delivery. You need to be bringing a better, or equal, quality product at a preferable better, or at least equal, price, or he won't be interested. If you're bringing a significantly more expensive product to the table, you had better understand that your presentation needs to focus on why your product will reduce his problems and make it worthwhile to spend more money. Everyone's motivation hinges on not having problems with your product. And everyone's motivation hinges on making their bosses and their customers happy. We visited a customer recently and found that a particular product he was purchasing was giving him headaches: missed deliveries primarily. When a supplier misses a promised delivery, everything down the chain suffers and who gets blamed? The purchasing agent of course.

And how did we find out his motivations to purchase (or change suppliers)? Asking questions--trying to get into his head. Ask questions. Get into your customer's head. Understand his/her motivation.

The Ninth Rule: Remember your Customer's most prized possession: their name

Remembering a customer's name may be one of the most important assets a salesperson may cultivate. What is the secret? First, you have to care about the person you are meeting. What it means to me when someone forgets my name, within minutes after being introduced, is that he doesn't care. Remembering a name is caring about the person you're being introduced to. "But I have a bad memory for names." Bad, bad excuse. The trick to remembering a name is to use it often in the first five minutes of being introduced.

"Ed, nice to meet you. Ed, what is it that you do? Who is it that you're here to see, Ed?"

Over and over, repeat the name in every sentence. And make an association with the name and person. Hair color; interesting characteristics, etc.

And, if you missed the name at the introduction, immediately say that "I'm sorry. I missed your name. I wasn't paying attention." It's easier to do this right away, then an hour later. And, when you call on someone who should probably know your name--DON'T ASSUME THEY DO. Say your name again. "Hey, Sal. It's Ed. Good to see you again." Don't put your customer in the awkward position that they have to admit they don't remember you.

The Tenth Rule: Turn your Smartphone Off!

The accounting firm, Deloitte, recently studied smartphone usage. There are 310 million smartphones used in the U.S. They found that the overall average times a person checked his phone during the day was 46. I suspect, however, that a salesperson checks his phone about 100 times a day.

The absolute worst thing a salesperson can do in the presence of a customer is to check his cell phone during a sales call or presentation. Even if you're not the primary presenter, you should never consult your phone unless it is directly related to a question asked by the customer, after asking for permission.

Turn your cellphone off; leave it in the car; do NOT consult your cellphone in the presence of a customer. This is the epitome of disrespect.

The Eleventh Rule: Be aware of your body language

If there is anyone reading this who thinks that body language is NOT critical to the selling process, they will never be successful. It is that simple. Body language can make or break the sale. Harvard psychologist, Amy Cuddy, has written a book called "Presence: Bringing Your Boldest Self to Your Biggest Challenges" (Little, Brown Spark, 1976). The message is very simple: Stand tall, like a superhero, hands on your hips, chest out, chin high, for two minutes before your meeting, and you will present yourself as powerful and knowledgeable."

I know this to be true. I made a sales call to a body shop. The owner was not there and his manager-wife greeted me. Despite being short, she stood tall and gave me a strong handshake. This was a woman in charge.

You cannot make a sale if you're hunched over and sad faced when you greet a customer.

I attended a rock concert recently. One of the acts was The Band Perry. The band has four members: Just based on body language, I ranked the lead singer as number 1, the backup violinist/keyboardist as number 2, the younger brother as 3, and the older brother as number 4. The older brother's body language was: "I don't belong here; I'm not as talented as my sister and brother and they are just letting me be here--to satisfy the family." The lesson from Amy Cuddy is to spend two minutes, in private, before any meeting, standing like a superhero: hands on your hips, chin high, focused. Then, go to your meeting smiling, strong handshake and confident.

This will get you the sale.

The Twelfth Rule: Always be Closing

What does it take to be a good closer? I can count on one hand the incredible closers I've experienced in 41 years. What did they do that was different from what the rest of us do?

1. **Confidence:** Good closers have absolute confidence that they provide the best solution to the customer. And they convey that confidence. I say best "solution," not necessarily the best product. Two people may be selling the same product, but the closer shows the customer that the

complete solution comes only from them. That is: confidence in yourself, confidence in your product, and, most importantly, confidence in your solution. This may extend to delivery, installation and aftermarket service as all part of the solution. The customer has to be convinced that you're with him all the way: order, shipment, installation, service, warranty. That's what the closer convinces the buyer that they're the best at the total solution.

2. **Follow up.** Big decisions are not made immediately. A good closer follows up and tries to determine what the objections to a decision may be by getting into the head of the buyer--and then provides answers to these objections. The sales process for the good closer is not over after the presentation.

3. **Persistence.** Good closers are not worrying about "bothering" the buyer. They must be sensitive to the buyer's request ("don't call me until next week"), but they never neglect the follow up. The buyer said "next week," you better call next week.

closers NEVER stop closing until the purchase order is signed.

The Thirteenth Rule: Embrace AI

The very words "artificial intelligence" (AI) strikes fear in most people. But, as I've said several times in this book, selling is a fine art and not easily duplicated if it is done right: deep productknowledge of your product and your competitors'; a well-practiced ability to state the value of your product in a few sentences as well as in a long sales presentation; the use of "fact-to-fact" technique rather than emails and text messages.

I have been working with AI for the past couple of years and I've watched it grow in capabilities—but it is nowhere near the capability of a salesperson grounded in their product knowledge and able to do face-to-face selling. That being said, AI can enhance your product knowledge and allow you to learn more about your product and make a better presentation.

Let's take and example: I asked Microsoft Copilot to explain the advantages of a Sub-Zero Refrigerator over a Maytag. Here's the response from Copilot:

"Sub-Zero refrigerators are often recognized for their high-quality components, superior craftsmanship, and longevity. They are designed to last for 20 years or longer, which is a testament to their durability. Some of the key advantages of Sub-Zero refrigerators include:

Dual Compressors: Sub-Zero refrigerators typically feature dual compressors, which means the refrigerator and freezer have separate cooling systems. This helps maintain optimal temperature and humidity levels for each compartment, leading to better food preservation.

Air Purification: Many models come with air purification systems that remove ethylene gas, odors, and bacteria, keeping food fresher for longer periods[2].

Vacuum Seals: Sub-Zero units often have vacuum seals which provide a tighter seal around the door, further enhancing the preservation of food.

Design Flexibility: Sub-Zero offers a variety of designs, including panel-ready options that allow for seamless integration into kitchen cabinetry for a custom look.

While I don't have specific comparative details about Maytag refrigerators, Maytag is known for producing reliable appliances at a more affordable price point. They offer a range of refrigerators with different features that might be more suitable for those who are looking for cost-effective solutions without the need for the advanced features that come with Sub-Zero models.

Choosing between Sub-Zero and Maytag will depend on your personal preferences, budget, and the specific features you value in a refrigerator. If you prioritize longevity, design flexibility, and advanced preservation technology, Sub-Zero might be the better choice. However, if you're looking for a reliable refrigerator at a more accessible price point, Maytag could be a suitable option."

Wow! That's very impressive. Now, I can go a step further and find out the benefits of my competitors and do a comparison. Using AI, I can be a better salesperson with much more product knowledge. I'm totally ready to sell Sub-Zero fridges.

Next, I asked Copilot to compare the Kia Sportage with the **Subaru Outback:** "The Subaru Outback and Kia Sportage are both popular SUVs, but they offer different advantages that might make one more suitable for you than the other. Here are some advantages of the Subaru Outback over the Kia Sportage based on various sources:

Standard Features: The Subaru Outback generally comes with more standard features compared to the Kia Sportage, which can provide more value for your money.

Performance: The Outback often has better handling and power, which can make for a more responsive and enjoyable driving experience.

All-Weather Capabilities: Subaru Outback's all-wheel drive is standard, making it well-suited for various driving conditions and ideal for outdoor enthusiasts.

Towing Capacity: The Outback has a higher towing capacity, making it a better option for pulling heavier loads.

Interior Space: The Outback typically offers more legroom for front passengers, which can be a significant advantage for taller drivers and passengers.

Fuel Economy: The Outback may offer better fuel economy, leading to fewer stops at the gas station.

It's important to consider your specific needs and preferences when choosing between these two SUVs. If you prioritize features like standard all-wheel drive, towing capacity, and interior space, the Subaru Outback might be the better choice. However, if you're looking for a vehicle with a lower starting MSRP and similar capabilities, the Kia Sportage could still be a great option. Always consider taking a test drive and reviewing the latest models and their features before making a decision."

Copilot also provides footnotes so that you can reference the sources for the statements.

Okay, let's raise the level of complexity a little. I asked Copilot to compare Ingersoll Rand air compressors with Sullair air compressors and got this response:

"When comparing Ingersoll Rand and Sullair rotary screw compressors, both brands are well-regarded in the industry, but they have distinct features that may make one more suitable for certain applications than the other. Here are some comparative advantages based on the information available:

Ingersoll Rand: Design and Build: Known for a cool-box design which helps prolong component life and a new paint process that improves resistance to corrosion.

Power Capacity: Offers a larger power capacity, which can be crucial depending on the application.

Noise Level: Tends to have a more compact design resulting in less operational noise.

Efficiency: Their two-stage airend offers up to 15% energy savings compared to single-stage compressors.

Sullair: Reliability: Established reputation for robust build and reliable performance, whether portable or stationary.

Innovation: Known for pioneering modern air compressor technology.

Performance: Provides more performance and efficiency in its horsepower range.

Customer Demand: Focuses on developing compressors that are more energy-efficient, quieter, and have a smaller footprint.

Ultimately, the choice between an Ingersoll Rand and a Sullair rotary screw compressor will depend on the specific requirements of your application, including power needs, space constraints, noise sensitivity, and efficiency considerations. It's recommended to consult with a specialist who can provide a detailed assessment based on your operational needs."

So AI definitely helps with gaining product knowledge. What is important is learning what kinds of prompts to use to make sure your question is specific enough.

How can AI be used as a tool to help us do a better job as sales professionals:

AI can be a powerful tool for salespeople, offering a range of capabilities that can enhance sales processes and outcomes. Here are some of the best ways a salesperson can use AI:

Lead Prioritization: AI can analyze large datasets to identify and prioritize the most promising leads, ensuring that sales efforts are focused where they are most likely to yield results. If you input a file of sales leads into Copilot, Copilot will prioritize the leads based on demographics and behavioral prediction. Best potential leads end up on top.

Personalization: By leveraging AI, salespeople can tailor their approach to each customer, using insights gleaned from data to personalize communication and offers.

Sales Forecasting: AI algorithms can predict future sales trends based on historical data, helping salespeople to set realistic targets and plan accordingly.

Efficiency in Tasks: AI can automate repetitive tasks such as data entry, scheduling, and follow-ups, freeing up time for salespeople to engage in direct selling activities.

Customer Insights: AI tools can provide deep insights into customer behavior by analyzing data from various touchpoints, enabling salespeople to understand customer needs better.

Email Management: AI can help manage and prioritize emails, highlighting the most important messages and suggesting optimal times for follow-up.

Enhanced Collaboration: AI can identify connections between colleagues and important contacts, facilitating better teamwork and knowledge sharing.

Data Enrichment: AI can pull in relevant data from third-party sources to enrich customer profiles within a CRM, providing a more complete view of each customer.

So I tested CoPilot on myself. I went to copilot.microsoft.com and asked about Ed Maxwell, someone I wanted to make a sales call on.

Here's the response I got:

"Ed Maxwell is the Chief Executive Officer (CEO) of Eastern States Associates, Inc., located in Palmer, MA. He has been a significant part of the company since joining his father in the business in 1975. Ed took over as president in 1990 and has been serving as CEO since 2010. His responsibilities include covering the New England territory alongside Tim and Rich.

Ed's interests extend beyond his professional life. He is passionate about music, kayaking, and biking. For over 25 years, he has been playing the upright bass for several community orchestras. Additionally, he enjoys playing the clarinet.

On a personal note, Ed's wife, Linda, is the CFO of Eastern States Associates, Inc. Together, they have three daughters and four grandchildren, making for a family deeply intertwined with the company's operations.

Eastern States Associates, Inc. was founded in 1955 by Edward Maxwell, Sr. The company is a manufacturer's rep agency that sells products through distribution to the retail petroleum industry as well as commercial and industrial whole-salers. Their product areas include fiberglass underground storage tanks, steel above ground tanks, air compressors, pumps, specialty piping, pressure vessels, canopies, and LED lighting.

For more detailed information or specific inquiries about Ed Maxwell or Eastern States Associates, Inc., you may contact the company directly at their Palmer, MA office."

This sketch gives any potential salesperson some pretty cool insights into me, my personality and my family. Excellent conversation starters.

AI is the future and will only become more and more important in the as it gets more and more sophisticated. Don't fear it, use it.

The Fourteenth Rule: Don't Be Afraid to Strike Out On Your Own

Manufacturers' Representatives ("Reps") are salespeople who operate as independent contractors and represent two or more manufacturers. Reps operate in a fixed territory and are usually under an exclusive contract for a specific territory. Reps can operate alone or in groups. Some Rep Agencies are medium sized corporations where the corporation has the contract with the manufacturer and the salespeople are employees.

I have spent my whole sales career as a Rep. Our agency has

10 field salespeople and we operate in several states. I love the independence.

Manufacturers seek out reps because reps work on commissions and only receive their commissions after the product has been sold and paid for. Rather than pay a sales employee a salary and expenses, the manufacturer pays the rep or the rep agency a commission only when the product is sold and paid for. This reduces the up-front costs of manufacturing.

Typical reps will represent products that are synergistic—related to each other—so that we can make one call and present several products from different manufacturers to the same customer. (Remember the Long Tail Theory discussed earlier? Reps typically have one or two "hit" products, and several "niche" products that reduce the cost of a sales call.)

For example, a rep may call on restaurants and sell a brand of drinking glasses, utensils, restaurant tables, chairs, etc.

Another rep make call on hair salons and sell scissors, shampoo, etc. etc.

Our rep agency specializes in products used by petroleum marketers like gas stations.

If you have confidence in your sales skills and have a passion for a particular area, check it out. Go to the Manufacturers' Agents National Association (MANA): www.manaonline.org.

Good salespeople are always in demand.

CHAPTER SIXTEEN

PostScript: The Master Salesperson

I had the great fortune of being mentored in sales by a master salesman, who also happened to be my father.

I have asked myself many times what the traits were that made him so successful. For one thing, he loved the sales process. It didn't really matter to him what he was selling--a $2 grease tip for a grease gun or a $150,000 oil water separator for an oil terminal--he sold everything with the same degree of enthusiasm. The commission dollars resulting from the sale didn't motivate him. The sales process motivated him; closing the deal motivated him.

We would attend trade shows and someone outside his territory would come up to him and start asking questions. He didn't slough the guy off to the salesman responsible; he made the sale, enthusiastically.

My first job out of graduate school was teaching in college. After 5 years I looked at my department chairman--the most unenthusiastic person on the face of the earth, and I looked at my father who was the same age and who lived each day full of enthusiasm. I asked myself who do I want to be like when I'm in my 50s and 60s. I left teaching to join my father and have not regretted it and at age 80 I'm still enthusiastic about my job. So I made a good decision.

So, enthusiasm for the sale and the sales process is one key ingredient.

My father was the ultimate relational salesman. His whole career as a salesman was building relationships. Relationships he carried for his whole life even after he retired. His customers were his true friends and they knew it was real.

I believe in relationship selling because my father, my mentor, was very successful because of this style. Build relationships and stop focusing on the order and you will have a success- ful sales career.

One story that my father used to tell—a story that said it all about his style—was about when he sold grease guns and other equipment to auto parts stores in the 1950's. His territory was

Connecticut and NY (Long Island). He would travel every week to a different part of his territory. There was one call he made on Long Island where the owner of the auto parts store would turn him away, month after month, year after year. One day, he went into the store and the owner said "take out your order pad" and he gave him a huge parts order. When my father asked "why now"? His response was that he wanted to see if my father would have the persistence to wait for the order. He became my father's biggest customer.

Never give up.

ABOUT THE AUTHOR

Fifty years ago, after receiving my PhD from Northwestern University and having spent five years teaching, I looked at who I wanted to be as I grew old. I saw my father, who embodied the passion and excitement of the sales profession, and decided that he was the person I wanted to be. I am not him. But I am still very excited and passionate about selling as he was.

Our company, Eastern States Associates, Inc., a manufacturers' rep agency, was his baby, and he allowed me to join him in 1975. As I was growing up, we never agreed on most things. But, all of a sudden, in 1975, he seemed very right. Did I change? Absolutely.

In 1980, Joe Flick (who is now the president of our company) joined us and he brought an incredible energy and hunger to our fledgling organization. Together, over the ensuing decades, Joe and I have grown our little company, weathered many storms, and stand tall and successful today.

Today, almost fifty years later, I am still as passionate about selling, as empathetic about our customers' needs, and as driven to learn more about our products every day.

Selling is a great profession.

INDEX

A

Alexa 71
Apologize 37
approach 27, 44, 46, 52, 62, 78, 85, 111, 160, 190

B

Belichick 58, 75, 76, 113, 132, 133
boss 1, 4, 20, 21, 32, 33, 79, 88, 95, 97, 99, 121, 142, 172, 173
Bots 70
business 3, 12, 27, 45, 46, 49, 50, 51, 52, 59, 60, 64, 68, 71, 73, 77, 78, 82, 93, 96, 100, 102, 109, 110, 111, 118, 132, 134, 136, 138, 142, 143, 149, 161, 165, 168, 169, 170, 191
Buyers 77, 78, 93

C

Chatbots 69, 71
Checklists 175
client 4, 17, 18, 19, 31, 34
Closing 60, 183
communication 2, 25, 42, 45, 64, 78, 190
competitive 3, 78, 97, 106, 134
confidence 12, 25, 26, 33, 59, 120, 128, 147, 160, 183, 184, 193
consistent 10, 50
Creating an Impact 34
creative 10, 40
customer 1, 12, 13, 16, 17, 18, 19, 20, 21, 23, 24, 25, 26, 27, 32, 33, 34, 35, 36, 37, 39, 41, 42, 43, 44, 45, 47, 48, 49, 50, 51, 53, 54, 55, 58, 60, 62, 63, 65, 68, 71, 72, 74, 75, 78, 79, 82, 85, 89, 90, 91, 93, 95, 96, 97, 98, 99, 100, 104, 109, 110, 111, 112, 113, 115, 119, 120, 121, 122, 123, 124, 126, 127, 132, 133, 134, 135, 136, 140, 141, 142, 143, 146, 149, 150, 153, 154, 155, 156, 157, 158, 159, 160, 161, 162, 164, 168, 169, 170, 171, 172, 173, 174, 175, 176, 177, 178, 179, 180, 181, 182, 183, 184, 190, 191, 193, 197

D

de-brief 144, 145
Delivery 33
Don't stop 172, 173

E

email 38, 39, 40, 63, 67, 103,
    105, 106, 107, 121,
    159, 170, 173, 174, 175
Email 38, 105, 173, 174, 175,
    190
emails 38, 43, 103, 104, 105,
    106, 121, 123, 152,
    170, 173, 174, 175,
    185, 190
empathy 2, 12, 15, 19, 33, 35
Empathy 4, 7, 15, 19
Engagement 34
enthusiastic 9, 26, 159, 196
equipment 17, 18, 96, 196
excuses 44, 81

F

Facebook 54, 71, 72, 73, 89,
    103, 155
Face to face 44, 45, 174
failure 4, 25, 76, 85, 113, 126,
    128, 129
Feedback and Adaptation 35
fight 63, 70
Fulfilling 10

G

Google 44, 54, 71, 82, 88, 89,
    104, 157, 174, 177, 178

H

handshake 111, 112, 132, 182,
    183
homework 55, 89
Hustle 59

I

Improvisation 34
information 26, 27, 41, 42, 46,
    63, 67, 69, 106, 136,
    137, 159, 167, 177,
    178, 188, 192
innovations 64
integrity 4
internet 63, 64, 65, 68, 69, 70
I will 4, 125, 147, 160

J

job seekers 2
journalist 11, 137

K

knowledge 3, 12, 23, 24, 25,
    26, 32, 33, 35, 36, 53,
    62, 68, 69, 72, 105,
    111, 113, 114, 115,
    119, 129, 134, 135,
    140, 142, 148, 151,
    153, 154, 160, 162,
    165, 176, 177, 185,

186, 189, 190

Knowledge 5, 7, 23, 25, 26,
   129, 134, 135, 153

L

Lazy 44
Lesson 75, 76, 83, 84, 85, 86
LinkedIn 39, 54, 64, 65, 72,
   73, 89, 90, 136
Luddites 64

M

Microsoft 68, 72, 185
Motivated 9

N

Never give up 76, 172, 197

O

office 18, 33, 92, 93, 99, 111,
   132, 133, 138, 142,
   149, 168, 192
online 43, 46, 52, 63, 117,
   118, 119
opportunities 4, 26, 59, 128
oxymoron 19

P

passion 9, 10, 11, 12, 19, 114,
   115, 160, 193
Passion VII, 4, 7, 9, 10, 12,
   13, 115, 159, 160
performance 31, 33, 34, 35,

74, 76, 122, 141, 143,
   144, 145, 148, 189
Phone 110, 174
pitch 16, 24, 32, 38, 39, 40,
   55, 61, 78, 86, 91, 97,
   113, 158
Power 188
preparation 33, 34, 78, 79, 96,
   97, 111
priority 4
product 10, 11, 12, 16, 17,
   18, 20, 23, 24, 25, 26,
   27, 32, 33, 34, 35, 36,
   39, 41, 45, 46, 47, 52,
   53, 60, 64, 67, 68, 69,
   72, 78, 79, 80, 82, 89,
   92, 93, 95, 97, 98, 99,
   100, 109, 111, 113,
   115, 119, 123, 124,
   126, 129, 130, 133,
   134, 135, 137, 140,
   141, 142, 143, 148,
   149, 151, 153, 154,
   155, 157, 159, 160,
   161, 162, 163, 164,
   165, 169, 171, 173,
   176, 177, 178, 179,
   180, 183, 184, 185,
   186, 189, 192, 193
Product 5, 7, 12, 23, 25, 62,
   114, 134, 140, 153,
   162, 176
psychological 2, 122

INDEX

Psychologists 19, 169

Q

question 34, 58, 75, 82, 111,
    137, 162, 182, 189

R

relationship 3, 45, 47, 50, 80,
    89, 95, 164, 196
robots 52, 68, 97, 117, 118

S

sale 18, 19, 26, 38, 44, 45,
    47, 48, 51, 53, 78, 79,
    80, 85, 88, 90, 91, 94,
    98, 100, 119, 125, 141,
    158, 160, 163, 164,
    172, 179, 182, 183,
    195, 196
sales 1, 2, 3, 4, 5, 10, 11, 15,
    19, 24, 27, 31, 32, 33,
    35, 36, 37, 39, 41, 42,
    44, 45, 46, 47, 48, 49,
    51, 53, 54, 58, 59, 61,
    62, 63, 64, 67, 68, 69,
    70, 71, 72, 73, 74, 75,
    77, 78, 81, 82, 83, 84,
    85, 86, 87, 88, 89, 91,
    95, 96, 97, 99, 100,
    101, 102, 103, 106,
    111, 112, 113, 114,
    118, 119, 120, 121,
    123, 124, 125, 126,
    127, 129, 130, 132,
    133, 134, 135, 136,
    138, 139, 141, 142,
    143, 144, 147, 149,
    150, 151, 152, 153,
    155, 156, 157, 158,
    160, 162, 163, 164,
    165, 168, 169, 171,
    172, 173, 177, 182,
    184, 185, 189, 190,
    191, 192, 193, 195, 196
Sales 2, 3, 29, 31, 45, 46,
    47, 48, 49, 81, 82, 91,
    99, 106, 117, 123, 126,
    130, 140, 142, 145,
    150, 151, 155, 158,
    164, 167, 170, 171, 190
salesman 26, 49, 62, 135, 149,
    159, 160, 195, 196
Salesmen 139
Salespeople 4, 25, 78, 86, 97,
    136, 137
salesperson 1, 4, 11, 12, 16,
    18, 19, 20, 23, 24, 25,
    26, 33, 34, 35, 36, 38,
    41, 44, 45, 47, 48, 49,
    50, 53, 59, 60, 61, 62,
    69, 72, 78, 79, 80, 81,
    84, 86, 88, 89, 91, 92,
    93, 94, 97, 98, 99, 100,
    106, 120, 122, 123,
    124, 125, 126, 128,
    136, 137, 139, 141,

203

143, 147, 151, 153,
154, 155, 156, 157,
161, 162, 163, 164,
165, 169, 175, 177,
178, 179, 180, 181,
182, 185, 186, 189, 192
Salesperson 44, 48, 88, 89, 97,
164, 195
Selling I, III, 1, 20, 53, 61,
126, 134, 149, 178
share 15, 118
Siri 44, 71
SMARTER 72
solution 1, 4, 18, 19, 20, 26,
54, 61, 62, 68, 78, 89,
95, 102, 105, 120, 154,
183, 184
student 4, 15, 16, 19, 62, 76
succeed 3, 4, 19, 59, 87, 115,
125, 126, 151
success 2, 4, 10, 12, 35, 72,
87, 95, 101, 102, 112,
113, 115, 127, 129,
134, 135, 142, 145,
146, 147, 162, 163, 165
survived 58

T

team 9, 48, 58, 59, 74, 75,
91, 102, 113, 131, 138

technologically 64
The Actor 33
The Grand Finale 35
The Script 33
The Stage 33

U

understand 3, 15, 16, 17, 18,
19, 20, 24, 26, 37, 41,
52, 62, 63, 65, 69, 71,
84, 85, 89, 91, 93, 96,
111, 113, 119, 134,
135, 137, 141, 143,
155, 157, 165, 174,
176, 179, 180, 190

V

Value Proposition 40, 51
volunteers 131

W

waiting 79, 150, 158
Wikipedia 51, 64, 134
Winners 112